Sep
1860

THE SWAMP

Also by Eric Bolling

WAKE UP AMERICA

Eric Bolling

THE SWAMP

**WASHINGTON'S MURKY POOL OF
CORRUPTION AND CRONYISM AND
HOW TRUMP CAN DRAIN IT**

ST. MARTIN'S PRESS ※ NEW YORK

www.stmartins.com

Designed by Jonathan Bennett

Front endpaper: July 1860, view of the incomplete Capitol Building. *(Courtesy of Library of Congress)*
Back endpaper: Circa 1860s view of the Capitol Building. *(Courtesy of Library of Congress)*

The Library of Congress Cataloging-in-Publication Data is available upon request.

ISBN 978-1-250-15018-9 (hardcover)
ISBN 978-1-250-15019-6 (ebook)

Our books may be purchased in bulk for promotional, educational, or business use. Please contact your local bookseller or the Macmillan Corporate and Premium Sales Department at 1-800-221-7945, extension 5442, or by email at MacmillanSpecialMarkets @macmillan.com.

First Edition: June 2017

10 9 8 7 6 5 4 3 2 1

I am a "Deplorable" and I stand with you.

I dedicate this book to all "Deplorables."

The truck drivers, the nurses, the construction laborers,
the auto workers, the retail clerks, the veterans . . . and
all the rest of the great hardworking, God–loving Americans.
We Deplorables have been ignored by the D.C. establishment
on both sides of the aisle for decades. Now our voices will
be heard and President Donald Trump will drain
the Swamp for us, the Deplorables.

CONTENTS

ACKNOWLEDGMENTS

To my amazing family, who have always supported me and stood by me, Adrienne, Eric Chase, Tina Rosales. I am blessed and grateful to have you, I love you all very much.

To my friends Sergio Gor, Mark Fisher, Jen Starobin, Greg and Donna Mosing, your loyalty and commitment to my success has not gone unnoticed, I am deeply appreciative and thankful for all you have done for me.

To my Fox News family, including Rupert Murdoch, James Murdoch, Suzanne Scott, Dianne Brandi, Kimberly Guilfoyle, Kyle Nolan, Bob Beckel, Sean Hannity, Dana Perino, Juan Williams, and Greg Gutfeld. My entire show staff on *The Five, Cashin' in,* and the countless producers who have made me look great throughout the years! True professionals who have not only shaped news coverage but American history.

To my phenomenal book publishing team, George Witte, Todd Seavey, Sally Richardson, Jennifer Enderlin, David Rotstein, Tracey Guest, Joe Rinaldi, Laura Clark, and Karlyn Hixson. You have all been incredibly supportive, helpful, and amazing to work with! You set the standard for excellence in your industry and beyond!

To all my loyal fans and the View Crew! You are the reason America will be GREAT again, President Trump will succeed and together we will drain the Swamp!

THE SWAMP

1. INTO THE MIRE

Integrity is the lifeblood of democracy. Deceit is a poison in its veins.
—SENATOR TED KENNEDY

We don't know exactly what went through thirty-seven-year-old Senator Ted Kennedy's mind the night of the Chappaquiddick crash. We can guess he was acutely aware of having a smart, athletic twenty-eight-year-old woman in the passenger seat beside him in the car. It wasn't just lust, he may have told himself. Mary Jo Kopechne was a charming rising star among his cadre of young staffers. In the prominent senator's mind, it was only natural to want some time alone with her. And perhaps he assumed that she would want to spend some time with him: the scion of America's legendary political dynasty.

He may still have been thinking happily of the party he'd just left behind, where five other married men like himself were partying with five of Mary Jo's young, single female friends, with alcohol flowing freely. Ted probably didn't think too much about his mother, who owned the car he was now driving, or the family chauffeur he'd left back at the party.

He was a U.S. senator. He was a Kennedy. He was invincible.

He should have given more thought to the darkness and rain that

July night in 1969, and to the slightly confusing layout of the road connecting the island of Chappaquiddick to Edgartown on the mainland of Massachusetts.

He stopped at the side of the road for a short time, confused by the route ahead, physically or morally. When he saw a cop approaching the car from behind, the reality of his situation may have come flooding back to him for a moment: It might look bad, a six-year senator from a powerful, high-profile family parking in the dark with a young beauty who admired liberal politicians and had worked for a few, including Ted's brother Robert, assassinated just a year earlier.

But this was no time to think of death, just of getting back to Edgartown and the hotel. Ted depressed the accelerator, bungled the shift for a moment, and lurched backward toward the cop. Not good. More shifting and the car rolled forward. The cop wandered off, and Ted drove forward, his path seemingly clear for a minute.

But the bridge at Chappaquiddick met the island's shore at an odd angle. It wasn't fair, really. Had Ted done anything so wrong? Had he done anything that a man of his stature wasn't entitled to do?

The car lurched and, for a sickening moment, seemed to hang in the air, then plunged into the narrow channel between Chappaquiddick and Edgartown. So narrow. So small. Yet it would separate Ted from all his ambitions to rise to an office higher than the one he held. How wrong it seems to members of the political class that such petty inconveniences can trip them up.

The car sank into the muddy channel bottom, wheels upward. Water rushed in immediately, and Ted thought with panic about how to save himself. He managed to get out the window. He rose to the surface and floundered over to the bank of the channel, near the bridge.

Ted later testified that he sat on the bank for a while, catching his breath, then began calling for Mary Jo. He shouted her name several times, he said, and got no response. He also testified that he tried several times to swim down to the car, to no avail.

Then, he did what any responsible member of the political elite might do. He decided to go back to the party—but first sat on the bank for about fifteen minutes, wondering if there were some way to keep all this from turning into a scandal. The political elite have learned to live with a great deal of ambient immorality. Scandal, though, is something to be avoided. The public should not get too long a glimpse of what lurks below the surface of the Swamp in the world of politics.

Ted trudged back to the party cottage, neither using a nearby pay phone to call the authorities nor stopping to ask for help at any of several cottages he passed, not even the one with a light on.

Perhaps Ted was in shock from the accident. Or perhaps the specter of death had ceased to hold much fear for this latest ill-fated member of the Kennedy clan. By that night, when Ted stumbled back to the Chappaquiddick party cottage, four of his eight siblings had already met untimely ends, best known among them President John F. Kennedy and his attorney general, Robert, both taken down by assassins.

Ted was the great remaining hope of the family.

At that very same moment that Ted reentered the party cottage, his brother John's loftiest ambition was reaching posthumous fruition as *Apollo 11* made its way from Earth to the moon, having launched just two days before Ted's crash. The astronauts would successfully travel 239,000 miles and back. Ted only had to navigate the length of an eighty-foot bridge at Chappaquiddick and in all likelihood he would one day have gone on to win the presidency, buoyed by the nation's desire to recapture the romanticized Kennedy glory days. It was not to be.

Back inside the party cottage, where less than an hour earlier he had borrowed car keys from Crimmins, his family chauffeur, Ted was careful not to alert the others to the circumstances from which he had just dragged himself. He said later he didn't want to alarm Mary Jo's friends, nicknamed the Boiler Room Girls, veterans of his brother Robert's truncated presidential campaign.

We can only speculate how they might have reacted to word of Mary Jo's accident. They might well have saved her life, though. A local fire department diver, John Farrar, would later testify that Mary Jo did not appear to have been killed by the initial crash but to have been trapped in a small and slowly shrinking pocket of air inside the car. She may still have clung desperately to life, hoping for rescue, even as Ted was asking himself how best to keep the whole thing quiet.

Ted still didn't call for help from the party cottage. Instead, he collected two of the other male party guests—his cousin Joseph Gargan and Gargan's friend Paul Markham, a former U.S. attorney. Together, without alerting the women present and without alerting the authorities, they went back to the scene of the crash, where both Gargan and Markham repeated the failed effort to dive down and find Kopechne in the wreck.

The two also tried in vain to convince the sobbing and panicked Ted that he had to contact authorities immediately. Ted told the two men to go back and attend to the other women at the party, that he would alert authorities. He did not.

Instead, apparently still possessing a good deal of physical energy, Ted swam across the five-hundred-foot channel to Edgartown, Massachusetts, part of Martha's Vineyard and the location of his hotel. The channel swim must have been strangely invigorating and meditative. For a few minutes, he had no moral or political responsibilities, just the almost-instinctive impulse to put hand ahead of hand, kick left and kick right, keep head above water and make it to welcoming land on the other side, a bit farther away from the disaster on the Chappaquiddick shore.

Ironically, Ted was quite comfortable around water. He was competing in the Martha's Vineyard yacht races that very week, another emblem of membership in the closest thing America has to aristocracy. Safety guidelines say alcohol shouldn't be used in cars or by people operating boats. Tradition says that drinking and yachting go together just fine.

Soaking wet, Ted made his way to his Edgartown hotel room and collapsed into bed, rising once at about 3:00 A.M. to complain to hotel management about a loud party. The fools had no idea how fitful his sleep was already, without them further disturbing him. You would think that if you had just driven your car off a bridge— likely drowning a young girl (not your wife)—and left the scene, the last thing you'd do would be to complain about some noise in the back hallway of your hotel. Then again: You're not a Kennedy.

In the morning, Ted was back in his element. All seemed almost right with the world as he chatted in the hotel with the winner of the previous day's yacht race. Ted felt a fleeting moment of envy. Yesterday was not a victory for him, and the consequences could not be avoided forever. It was now the morning of July 19, 1969.

Ted was joined at the hotel by Gargan and Markham, and he argued with them about his reasons for not yet contacting authorities. The three then took a ferry back to Chappaquiddick Island, where they found no sign that Kopechne had miraculously survived, and so Ted used a pay phone to make several phone calls.

Unbelievably, however, the calls still weren't to the authorities.

Instead, Ted called several friends, asking for their advice. Apparently, he was not yet persuaded by the consensus in favor of him reporting the incident to police. There had to be some way out of this waking nightmare. The rain and dark of the previous night could not possibly be allowed to shatter the sunlit world of a happy, smoothly functioning Martha's Vineyard. After all, he had a yacht to race. There had to be a solution. He was a Kennedy. There was always a solution.

But by this time, fishermen had spotted the wrecked car and called police, who summoned professional divers to retrieve Kopechne's body. When Ted heard the growing island chatter suggesting that the authorities had already intervened, he realized he must at least keep up appearances of striving to do the right thing. The basic formalities must be given their due, the polite outer forms given a nod. That might yet do the trick. There was no bringing Mary Jo Kopechne back to life, much as Ted had genuinely hoped the whole situation would somehow be rectified by morning with the miraculous appearance of Mary Jo alive and well on another shore—but at least the life of Ted Kennedy might yet be salvaged.

That counted for a great deal, at least in his mind.

Ted headed to the Edgartown police station, while his cousin Gargan went to the party cottage to tell the remaining Boiler Room Girls about the prior night's crash. Ted told police in a statement that he had been in shock after the accident, that he recalled curling up in the back of a car parked near the party cottage, then walked around a bit before returning to his Edgartown hotel and "immediately" contacted authorities in the morning upon realizing what had happened.

At trial one week later, Kennedy pleaded guilty to leaving the scene of an accident and received the minimum possible sentence— two months—which was suspended, his sterling prior reputation supposedly a motivating factor in the lenient punishment. His driver's license was suspended for a year and a half—a terrible hardship for ordinary Americans but not that devastating when you have a chauffeur such as Crimmins at your disposal.

In January 1970, an inquest was held to determine the cause and manner of Mary Jo's death. It was performed in secret, and the transcript was not released until after the grand jury had met. The judge said Kennedy was "probably negligent," but the district attorney chose not to prosecute. Three months later, a grand jury was convened. The DA said there was not enough evidence to indict Kennedy, and the grand jury agreed. And so the most prominent member of the Kennedy clan went free to party on Martha's Vineyard another day.

Somehow, Ted would remain a standard-bearer, and a senator, for another forty years after the crash, until his own death in 2009.

Mary Jo Kopechne, who died one week shy of her twenty-ninth birthday, had been responsible for a campaign region that included her birth state of Pennsylvania. After growing up in New Jersey and getting a business administration degree from that state's Caldwell College for Women, Kopechne moved to Alabama, participating in the civil rights movement, and soon to Washington, D.C.—then still seen as a beacon of hope and locus of reform by so many well-meaning young people. After a short stint with Florida senator George Smathers, she became part of the secretarial staff for Robert Kennedy, U.S. senator from New York, admired by so many young liberals as the rightful inheritor of the torch that had been carried by his brother John until John's assassination.

After Robert was assassinated as well, Kopechne might well have experienced enough Kennedy-related tragedy for one lifetime. But there was one more act to be performed, one that would make her story forever part of that political clan's checkered tale.

In his statements to the press, Ted claimed he had not been drinking the night of the crash—and some in the press pretended for years to believe him. His son, former congressman Patrick Kennedy, has asserted in recent interviews that Ted was killed by his severe alcoholism and that he hid prescription medications where he could get them at any time for recreational use and kept vodka in his water bottles. (Familial bad habits would be handed down from father to son, it seems, since Patrick Kennedy fought his own battles with prescription medicine abuse, alcohol, and reckless driving while serving in Congress, eventually compensating by becoming an antimarijuana crusader.)

Back in 1969, Ted's wife Joan, herself an admitted alcoholic, attended the Kopechne funeral with him, doing her duty and standing by him. Joan had a miscarriage, her third, shortly thereafter and blamed it on stress from the controversy surrounding Chappaquiddick. She stuck with Ted a good while longer, though, before finally divorcing him thirteen years later, in 1982.

This deeply flawed man somehow made it through decades of rather restrained press scrutiny with almost no reckoning for his actions at Chappaquiddick—save the lingering distrust that kept the public from entrusting him with the highest office in the land. He declined to run in 1972 and 1976 despite his high political profile, then failed to secure the Democratic nomination in 1980 when he briefly hoped, perhaps, that the taint of scandal was behind him.

He remained in the Senate until his death twenty-nine years later, regarded as one of its philosophical and intellectual leading lights by many liberals—pleased by his big-spending ways and go-it-alone moves like attempting to negotiate peace with the Russians in defiance of the wishes of then-president Ronald Reagan, an act seen by conservative critics as tantamount to treason. In the wake of that criticism, he urged the voters of Massachusetts to consider whether they thought him still fit to represent them, but he did not resign. He campaigned, usually winning easily, every six years for the rest of his life.

The real issue, though, is not Ted Kennedy's dubious policy judgments, nor even the precise time line of events that July in Chappaquiddick, but why, time and again, we look to the political figures in Washington as if they are moral leaders. Given the shocking number of politicians and bureaucrats involved in ethical and legal violations, we might be closer to the truth if instead of seeing them as moral exemplars, we thought of them as a criminal class, dwelling in a moral swamp of their own making, from which saner citizens wisely steer well clear.

Neither Kennedys nor Congress members are an aristocracy born to rule us, or even to give us sound advice.

In fact, in 2000, at a time when Patrick Kennedy was chairman of the Democratic Congressional Campaign Committee, the police-reporting site Capitol Hill Blue did a study of then-current Congress members' arrest records and reported that twenty-nine had been accused of spousal abuse, seven had been arrested for fraud, nineteen had been accused of writing bad checks, one hundred and seventeen had bankrupted at least two businesses, three had been arrested for assault, seventy-one were unable to qualify for credit cards, and eight had been arrested for shoplifting.

Much as we might like to imagine politicians have higher standards than the rest of us—since, after all, they're so often the ones lecturing the rest of us about what to do—this book will show that they are a good deal worse than you and I.

Oh, and Ted is hardly alone in having trouble behind the wheel. Capitol Hill Blue's survey found that in 1998 alone, 84 out of 535 members of Congress had been stopped for drunk driving. But in all cases, they were released by the loyal United States Capitol Police after claiming congressional immunity. So long as members of Congress claim they are headed to the Capitol to vote and do the people's business, they cannot be jailed along the way. They might kill someone, of course, but they mustn't be stopped from governing us.

No single day in history is sufficient to indict our entire system of government, but the Chappaquiddick crash was not as unusual as it first appears. Ethical violations are daily business in the swamp that is D.C. Not all the creatures dwelling in the D.C. swamp are char-acters with as much panache as the Kennedy clan, but that doesn't make the rest of the Swamp any more pleasant, as I'll explain.

Would you believe that during the Obama years a U.S. dis-trict court judge was arrested trying to buy cocaine from an FBI agent? Or that another was sentenced to jail for two years for lying about sexual harassment? Or that a New York congressman did jail time for tax fraud? Or that a California congresswoman was fined $10,000 for tampering with evidence related to campaign violations?

In just the past few years, members of Congress have also been found guilty of fraud, drunk driving, and racketeering. During these years, a congressional communications director became the first per-son ever convicted of lying to the Office of Congressional Ethics, though it is a safe bet these were not the first lies told in D.C.

During these years, a former Speaker of the House pleaded guilty to paying hush money in order to cover up sex with underage boys. Members of Congress resigned after soliciting sex on Craigslist, having multiple staffers collect fraudulent reelection-petition signa-tures, sending women lewd pictures, and making unwanted sexual advances. Officials of the General Services Administration, which is supposed to keep careful track of federal government procurements, were fired or resigned over a fun-filled $800,000 weekend at tax-payer expense in Las Vegas.

The litany of these scandals is in turn dwarfed by the better-known gunrunning, terror-attack-bungling, IRS-corrupting, veterans-neglecting, and data-stealing mishaps that characterized the eight years of Obama's presidency. Those incidents had bigger consequences, but the quiet bubbling of the Swamp—and its usual sexual and financial escapades—goes on in the background, year after year, numbing us to the bigger disasters when they come along.

Read on to find out who all the scoundrels mentioned above are and how the Washington political culture that helped create them works.

What Ronald Reagan saw as a "Shining City" (or at least the capital city of the metaphorical shining city that is America) in fact sits atop a literal swamp, as if its very foundations were evil, like those of the house in *Poltergeist*. Washington is a city of no-bid contracts and general cronyism despite the constant pretense of scrupulous ethics rules and press watchfulness. And it didn't just get this way recently. The Swamp wasn't created by this year's batch of Democrats or by eight years of Obama, nor by the 1960s decadence during which the Chappaquiddick crash happened. It has been this way since the earliest days of the republic, though in many ways it has grown exponentially worse.

Politicians are not demons but neither are they angels, and they are prone to the same vices as the rest of humanity, writ larger and more dangerous by the vast power and the vast resources with which they are entrusted. Time and again, as was likely the case at Chappaquiddick, sex plays a role in their moral stumbles, and we take a look at that troubling pattern next.

2. SEX IN THE SWAMP

I did not have sexual relations with that woman.

—BILL CLINTON

There may be some deep psychological connection between the impulse that drives people to seek political power and the impulse to manipulate the young and vulnerable, even though to most of us, the powerful would seem to have nothing left to prove—and better ways to prove it even if they felt compelled to show off.

What goes through the mind of someone like President Bill Clinton when he jeopardizes everything by receiving oral sex from a White House intern?

Maybe with every "bimbo eruption" of the Clinton presidency, Bill lived on some unconscious level and felt that he was accomplishing the same thing he does when impressing a crowd with a speech or getting votes: compensating for a youth of absent or emotionally distant relatives, a youth driven by the need for affirmation and support.

Bill Clinton is famously the son of a traveling salesman who died three months prior to Bill's birth. Then his mother moved to New Orleans for nursing school, leaving him to be raised for a few years by his grandparents. When his mother returned, she married an alcoholic car dealership owner who abused her and Bill's brother, forcing Bill to fight him at times.

Away from home, though, Bill found the affirmation that came with high school public speaking and a teenage visit to the Kennedy White House. He decided to study law and in law school found his lifelong partner, Hillary Rodham, who would both support him in his political ambitions and tolerate his craving for ever more female attention. It wasn't hard to find by the time he was seated in the Arkansas governor's mansion, as attested to by witnesses ranging from state troopers who looked the other way during Bill's sexual rendezvous to the multiple women, some working in government, who would accuse him of inappropriate sexual advances.

He was probably pleasantly surprised the first time a twenty-two-year-old, unpaid White House intern named Monica Lewinsky offered to show him her thong underwear, but it wasn't the first time the emptiness inside him that never quite is filled would compel him to forget about Hillary and the duties of office for just a little while.

He would have been surprised but not shocked. Impressionable and ambitious young women are often swayed by proximity to power, and he simply couldn't be expected to forgo the dizzying possibilities that dynamic offered. Bill told the public he never inhaled when he smoked pot, but he knew the addictive power of illicit sex. What was one more? And she seemed smart. Happy. Cute in that plump Middle American way Bill liked.

As long as the public didn't know, he was fine. Prerogatives of office. And Hillary wouldn't care, not really—not unless his behavior jeopardized his presidency and thus their shared power. That would anger her. Enough to send her into furious screaming rages, some say. But there was no way this delightful secret moment—which soon became multiple encounters—would become public.

Unless, of course, Bill were asked about the little affair under oath and made the mistake of lying about it.

But we'll revisit that disastrous moral and political miscalculation in a later chapter.

The very first person to start his presidency in the city of Washington, D.C.—the nation's third president, Thomas Jefferson—was the subject of sexual scandal a year after he took office, and it was a scandal that reverberates to this day.

Jefferson was a man of the Enlightenment, a rationalist who appreciated the symmetrical, radiating road plan surrounding the still-new Capitol Building in 1802, even if everything for miles around rested upon barely reclaimed swampland. George Washington and, for most of his administration, John Adams had governed from the stabler ground of Philadelphia and New York City, the two prior capital cities since the Constitution had gone into effect.

While Jefferson's head was in D.C., though, his heart was in nearby Monticello, Virginia, where one of his household slaves, Sally Hemings, had been his lover since she was fourteen, back in 1787, when Jefferson was forty-four. She had become his lover and, most experts now believe, had by 1802—the year the affair became a widespread public rumor—given birth to four of his children, two of them then still living, named Beverley and Harriet. Within a few years, there would be two more, sons named Madison and Eston. Such a relationship was not illegal but was frowned upon, less because of the obvious difference in power between the two lovers that troubles us today than because free people and slaves—and white people and black people—were not supposed to mix.

Making the whole relationship stranger, and reminding us how intimately and strangely slaves and owners were bound together before the Civil War, Sally was a half sibling of Jefferson's deceased wife, whose father had also taken a slave as his companion after his wife's death. Sally was three-quarters white—still not enough to make her born free when she came into the world two months after her father's death. Even in an era when a husband's legal authority over a wife was considerable, Jefferson would wield vastly more power over Hemings than he had over Martha Wayles Jefferson.

Still, historians agree that Jefferson and Hemings's relationship was likely a loving one, however disturbing it may be by modern standards. In theory, she could have escaped at the very time their sexual relationship likely began, when the then-recently widowed Jefferson was traveling with her in France, where slavery was illegal, in 1787. It would have taken great courage on her part to strike out alone.

And after all, while traveling in France, perhaps it was almost as if the two of them could forget about the fraught ethical problems of the young nation they had left behind across the Atlantic. France was then, for a short, fleeting time, technically a constitutional monarchy, to some admirers the Enlightenment ideal, and not yet the blood-soaked revolutionary battleground it would become in 1789.

So it was that the man who penned what may be the most important statement of individual rights and liberties in human history, the United States Declaration of Independence, through his ownership of slaves added to his legacy a line of familial descent that DNA tests in 1998 strongly suggest continues to our own day. The Jefferson-Hemings descendants are living embodiments of the double helix of greatness and moral failure that makes up our national political inheritance.

Jefferson freed what were almost certainly his own children as they came of age, though not his other slaves. We can't just chalk his moral error up to the times in which he lived, since some of the other Founding Fathers freed all their slaves, or never owned any in the first place. Jefferson was surely crafting an imperfectly philo-sophical document when he wrote the Declaration—like the con-sensus of state views that would become the Constitution eleven years after the Declaration was written—but maybe he projects a bit of guilt in the passage where he attempts to blame the thriving of the slave trade in the New World on King George III.

On that point, at least, Jefferson was not in much position to criticize.

The spread of rumors about the Jefferson-Hemings relationship in 1802 was the aftereffect of even earlier political scandals in the young republic. Jefferson had hired a Scottish political pamphleteer named James Callender to write denunciations of Jefferson's rival, the Federalist president John Adams, helping radical Jefferson to win the election of 1800 and turn the crusty Adams into the nation's first one-term president.

Unfortunately, Jefferson also hinted he would make Callender postmaster general—and reneged. Enraged, Callender made it his mission to spread reports of the surprisingly fair-skinned child slaves at Monticello. Despite the prevalence of heated political exchanges in the journals of the day, though, Jefferson never bothered to con-test the claims. That may be a testament to his affection for Hemings and their children, whom he never officially acknowledged but did not disavow.

In his strange way, Jefferson defied the systems of his day—ending monarchy in his homeland and loving across a master-slave divi-sion line that would not vanish for decades after his affair with Hemings. On the other hand, if you love somebody, set her free.

Two years after Jefferson's death at Monticello in 1826, his Democratic-Republican Party evolved into the Democratic Party that we know today. Its political philosophy has changed more than once since then, but it featured sex scandals almost from the outset—one that nearly destroyed the first Democratic presidency, that of

Andrew Jackson, a veteran of multiple wars and campaigns against the Native Americans, who became a legislator and then president.

Few political sex scandals had the historical ramifications of the so-called Petticoat Affair, between Jackson's secretary of war and a married woman that led to all of Jackson's other cabinet members resigning. Like Jackson himself, John Eaton was a former U.S. senator from Tennessee. Unlike the aged and experienced Jackson, Eaton, at twenty-eight, was the second-youngest person ever to serve as a U.S. senator. (In both his case and that of Virginia's Armistead Thomson Mason, who had served a few years earlier, voters were apparently willing to ignore the Constitution's requirement that a senator be thirty years old.)

In 1818, he befriended a navy purser named John Timberlake, who was ill-suited for the job of keeping track of ships' budgets. Timberlake was a drunkard and debtor. He had one thing going for him, though: his wife, Peggy, a renowned beauty and daughter of a prominent bar owner. By her own admission, she had learned to flirt and to enjoy the attention of men in her father's bar from a young age. Her father barely stopped her from eloping with an army officer when she was just a teenager. She married Timberlake a short time later but soon caught the eye of the young senator from Tennessee and may have become romantically involved with him.

When Eaton's attempt to persuade the Senate to legislate an end to Timberlake's debts failed, Eaton came up with another solution that had the convenient side effect of sending Timberlake very, very far away from his wife. Eaton found Timberlake a new, high-paid position with the navy's Mediterranean Squadron. There were rumors in Washington that it was all Eaton's way of having Peggy to himself. There were also rumors, when Timberlake died in 1828, that he had committed suicide, distraught at his wife having an affair with Eaton. The doctors said he died of lung disease and pneumonia.

That year also saw Jackson elected president, and despite the short mourning period since Timberlake's death, Jackson was quick to urge Eaton and Peggy to marry. On New Year's Day 1829, still two months before Jackson's inauguration under the procedures of the day, Peggy married Eaton, the man who would soon be secretary of war. In so doing, she earned the immediate enmity of the wives of the other cabinet members, who thought her mourning period too brief, hinting at a long-existing extramarital affair.

Peggy also found herself hated by Floride Calhoun, wife of Vice President John Calhoun, who became the ringleader of the anti-Peggy wives, attempting to ban her from elite parties and dinners and helping to spread the rumors of an Eaton affair in the press. It was a campaign of hostility made easier by the fact that Peggy was outspoken and uncouth. To some of the Washington elite, who imagined themselves paragons of proper behavior, she seemed as if she did not belong.

The conflict tore apart President Jackson's family, too. Because he was a widower, his niece played the role of official hostess for White House functions, but she also was part of the anti-Eaton faction, and so the loyal President Jackson dismissed her and replaced her with his daughter-in-law.

Secretary of State Martin Van Buren was spared some of this nonsense for the simple reason that he had no wife to join in plotting the intrigue. He became closer to Jackson as a result and was thus better positioned to run for president himself, as a successor to Jackson.

The anti-Peggy efforts backfired in another, more important way. Calhoun's acquiescence to his wife's role in the controversy was seen by the public as making him too divisive a figure to entrust with the presidency, which had been his long-term goal. Poor Peggy had her revenge.

Even before these events, though, Jackson found himself pitted against his vice president on multiple levels. Jackson continued to sympathize with Peggy in part because his own wife had been dogged by rumors that she had married him before she was legally divorced from her prior husband. Jackson was convinced that the stress caused by those rumors contributed to his wife Rachel's death just weeks after his election—and just two weeks prior to Eaton and Peggy marrying with Jackson's blessing.

The fraught Jackson-Calhoun personal relationship in turn meant heightened political tension between the two men during intense debates over tariffs (harmful to the South and referred to as the Tariff of Abominations) in the early 1830s, which led to the Nullification Crisis of 1832, an early version of the fundamental debate over whether states could constitutionally override the will of the federal government. That debate would not be settled until the Civil War—and perhaps still isn't completely settled.

Faced with ongoing public scandal over the cabinet infighting, Van Buren offered Jackson his resignation, and Jackson seized the opportunity to ask several other cabinet members, whom he held in much lower regard, to resign as well. Only the postmaster general stayed on, and the secretary of war who started the controversy, John Eaton, departed to become governor of the Florida Territory and later ambassador to Spain. He remained married to Peggy until his death in 1856, and she remarried three years later at age fifty-nine to an Italian dancer and music teacher.

She lived another twenty years and late in life summed up the tumult of her youth by saying, "I suppose I must have been very vivacious."

The nation was still struggling with the residual effects of slavery—and still home to various forms of institutionalized racism—three and a half decades after Peggy's death when, in 1915, President Woodrow Wilson did something that shocked the nation's sensibilities more than his Progressive, white-supremacist views.

The president began a romance a mere seven months after his first wife, Ellen Axson, died. He was soon engaged, and nine months after this scandalous romance began, he married for the second time, to the beautifully named Edith Bolling. Her great-grandmother had been one of Thomas Jefferson's sisters. (Edith herself had been married before, to a jeweler named Galt, who passed away in 1908.)

Edith was described by the press as "a ninth-generation descendant of Pocahontas" and enjoyed referring to herself as a "red Bolling."

In 1916, a year after the wedding, many of Wilson's advisors were worried that the quick remarriage could cost Wilson reelection.

What they should have been worried about was how quickly Wilson abandoned a far more important vow: He campaigned in 1916 on the slogan "He kept us out of war" as World War I raged across Europe. Yet just one month after his second inaugural, he sought and received Congress's declaration of war against Germany for its aggressive acts on the high seas against England and its allies.

Wilson's false promises echoed long after the war's end as well, since he inveigled Congress with the promise that this would be "a war to end all wars." It was not. Nonetheless, in 1919 he was awarded the Nobel Peace Prize, another reminder of how hollow that medal really is.

In the end, it may have been Edith who deserved a prize.

After being viewed with great suspicion by the press and political advisors, she ended up effectively being, in the estimation of some historians, our first female president. In the autumn of 1919, Wilson, exhausted by traveling to drum up support for the Treaty of Versailles (which ended one great war only to create the conditions leading to another), suffered a stroke that left him paralyzed and blind on his left side, with limited energy or capacity for the demands of the presidency. Edith made many decisions for him and selected which materials to bring to his attention for more than a year at the

end of his second term. He would live another three years after leaving office.

On May 10, 1924—three months after Wilson's death and nearly one
year after the death of Wilson's successor, Warren G. Harding—
President Calvin Coolidge appointed a new director of the Bureau
of Investigation. For the next forty-eight years, as the bureau
expanded and was renamed the Federal Bureau of Investigation, J.
Edgar Hoover would watch as presidents and members of Congress came and went, while he remained—and kept files.

Hoover was credited with bringing modern forensic and finger-
printing methods to the bureau, and they would aid the government
in fighting Prohibition-era gangsters, then Nazi spies, then Communist agents during the Cold War—and, as Hoover's power and
abuses of power grew, many peaceful antiwar and counterculture
groups. Along the way, a recurring interest of Hoover's was the
danger that government workers engaged in blackmailable activities,
such as homosexuality in those days, could be turned into national
security liabilities.

This was ironic, as it is likely Hoover himself was gay—and a
transvestite. He knew firsthand the power that could be held over
individuals by threatening to out their secrets in an intolerant
society—and used that power preemptively.

It wasn't just sex that people feared Hoover exposing. A year
before Hoover's death at age seventy-seven, Richard Nixon said that
one of the reasons Hoover was still working was that Nixon feared
the sorts of reprisals Hoover might inflict upon him if fired. Eventually, on May 2, 1972, time and nature got rid of Hoover without
Nixon needing to make a decision, but it didn't save Nixon's presidency, which would end two years later under investigation by the
FBI for the White House's role in the Watergate break-in.

In between his Al Capone–era start as director and his Nixon-era demise, Hoover played a role in convincing an otherwise tolerant President Eisenhower to issue his 1953 order banning gays and lesbians from working for any agency of the federal government, on the grounds that they could too easily be blackmailed and manipulated. In the name of keeping them from becoming pawns of the Communists, gays and lesbians became victims of their own government's snooping and persecution.

Just prior to Eisenhower's administration, President Harry S. Truman had warned that Hoover's FBI was becoming like a "Gestapo or secret police." Truman said, "They are dabbling in sex scandals and petty blackmail. J. Edgar Hoover would give his right eye to take over, and all congressmen and senators are afraid of him." (Truman, in retirement, expressed a similar worry about the CIA, when he wrote a letter to the editor at *The Washington Post* a few weeks after the Kennedy assassination, saying, "I never had any thought when I set up the CIA that it would be injected into peacetime cloak and dagger operations.")

Perhaps power went to Hoover's head. Even as he kept a suspicious eye on other people, he may have thought he could get away with odd behavior. Being a transvestite is no crime, but one anecdote about Hoover's purported transvestism suggests, at least, that he was very eccentric. There is no way to verify the claim, but Tim Gunn, the fashion consultant and TV personality, recounts (as reported by the site Jezebel) that when he was very young, in the 1950s or early '60s, he and his sister went to visit their father, an FBI agent, at the bureau's headquarters. Their father told them that in Director Hoover's office, they would find a very special guest: Vivian Vance, who played Ethel on *I Love Lucy*.

She said hello to the children and was very pleasant—and only years later did it occur to them that it would be odd for Vance to be in the FBI director's office. And only then did it occur to them that there was a striking resemblance between Vance—and J. Edgar Hoover.

Perhaps the young Gunns never really met Ethel that day.

Washington is full of people who behave oddly because they are intoxicated by their own power and by proximity to other people with power. A great deal of the time, they're also intoxicated in the more mundane sense of the word.

So it was with Representative Wilbur Mills, Democrat of Arkansas, on October 9, 1974, when his car was pulled over by U.S. Park Police, a fairly common experience for the political elite—except that Mills was not only drunk, his face was visibly injured due to a fight he'd been having with the car's other occupant, Argentine stripper Fanne Foxe (a.k.a. Annabelle Battistella), who leaped into the Tidal Basin in a failed attempt to escape the cops and was taken to the hospital.

Mills was not obscure enough in those days to hope that the incident would go unnoticed. He had been chairman of the powerful House Ways and Means Committee—the ultimate spenders of our tax dollars—for sixteen years and had been in the House since 1939. At age sixty-five, Mills was suddenly only two months away from retirement, but not on the schedule he had anticipated.

Incredibly, though, it was not this incident alone that finished Mills. A month later, he was reelected to his seat in Congress. A few weeks after that, perhaps made cocky by escaping political doom so quickly, Mills was involved in another incident.

On November 30, 1974, Mills stumbled onto the stage of a strip club in Boston where Foxe was performing—not with Foxe herself but with Foxe's apparently very forgiving husband. Mills then proceeded to give a very drunk press conference from Fanne Foxe's dressing room. It was probably a hell of a lot of fun at the time—

but shortly thereafter, Mills resigned first his chairmanship, then his seat in Congress. Then he joined Alcoholics Anonymous and checked himself into rehab.

That wasn't the end of him, though. He sobered up enough to find his way back to the Swamp and worked at a powerful D.C. law firm until about one year before his death in 1992.

At least Fanne Foxe, Mills's pal for decadent hijinks, was an adult.

Representative Donald "Buz" Lukens, Republican of Ohio, was caught on camera in 1989 in a McDonald's, talking to the mother of a sixteen-year-old girl about having sex with the daughter. Lukens was later accused of paying forty dollars and gifts to the mother for the sexual services of the daughter and accused of having begun the sexual relationship with the girl when she was only thirteen.

Technically, sex with the girl when she was sixteen was not a crime and the sex with her at thirteen unproven, but the fifty-eight-year-old congressman was charged in 1989 with "contributing to the delinquency of a minor." His appeal after conviction was built around destroying the reputation of the teenage girl, suggesting that he couldn't have significantly contributed to her delinquency, since she was already prone to misbehavior, including theft, running away, curfew violations, and mental health problems. Mental health problems are understandable in a young girl who's being pimped out by her own mother.

In 1991, Lukens would serve nine days of a thirty-day jail sentence for his crimes, but not before finishing out his time in Congress in colorful fashion. Despite the pleas of the Republican congressional leadership, he refused to resign but lost his 1990 Republican primary (to future Speaker John Boehner). He wasn't finished making an impression on his fellow members of Congress. With mere months to go in his final term, Lukens found himself being investigated by Congress for fondling a Capitol Building elevator operator. The day after the investigation began, in October 1990, he resigned.

The Washington elite are as irresponsible about sex as they are about balancing the federal budget.

Anthony Weiner seemingly had it all before he began misbehaving: political power, media buzz, and an attractive, intelligent wife—Hillary Clinton's influential right-hand woman, Huma Abedin—but he couldn't resist the urge to swap sexy texts with women, at least one of them underage.

The people of New York elected Weiner to Congress seven times, starting in 1998, and he remained there until his resignation in June 2011, which sadly did not come before he repeatedly vehemently denied sexting—sending sexual text messages and pictures—to women who were not his wife, Huma, in this case via the sometimes-public medium of Twitter, which was reckless to the point of seeming self-destructive. What's worse, though, is the eagerness with which the Democrats and the media repeated Weiner's claims that he must have been hacked and the sex-related messages sent out by someone trying to embarrass him. That was the story for a few short, strange days.

Of course, Weiner did not convincingly *deny* being that one indecent bulge depicted in the photo from his Twitter account. After three weeks of suggesting that he would weather the storm of controversy and carry on as a congressman, Weiner, still supported by a patient but unhappy-looking Huma, announced his resignation and admitted that there were in fact six women with whom he had exchanged sexy pictures over the preceding three years. From angry denials to complete surrender in a few short weeks.

And everyone thought that would be the last we'd hear from Anthony Weiner.

But he returned, astonishingly presuming to run for New York

City mayor in 2013—and allowing a film crew to record intimate details of his campaign for the later documentary *Weiner*. More astonishingly—unless we just accept that Weiner is an addict or a psychotic of some sort—he continued sexting even during this miracle comeback. The documentary crew, in a moment that would have left me, as a TV professional, positively perplexed, was present at Weiner campaign headquarters when news of the resumed sexting broke, and they got to see Huma's quite human rage as she told the crew to exit so she could have words with her husband in private. We will have to use our imaginations to picture Weiner explaining how he came to use the online alias "Carlos Danger" in his sexts to women such as twenty-two-year-old Sydney Leathers, who, despite the suggestive name, first contacted Weiner to tell him she *disapproved* of his sexting habits. Maybe Weiner likes a challenge.

Three years later, in 2016, when it came out that Weiner was not only still sexting but (inadvertently or not) appeared to have sexted an underage girl, Huma finally gave Weiner the boot, announcing her intention to separate from him. One can't help wondering whether it was really long-simmering exasperation with Weiner that drove Huma over the edge—or her awareness that her relationship with Hillary Clinton, who was then in the midst of her 2016 campaign for president, was ultimately more important and more lasting than her relationship with Weiner.

A month and a half after Clinton's defeat in that election, it was reported by *The Wall Street Journal* that federal prosecutors were considering child pornography charges against Weiner. The powerful are compelled to live dangerously, it seems—Carlos-dangerously in this case. There were also reports Weiner and Abedin, incredibly, might get back together.

The Clintons, of course, will be a story unto themselves in a later chapter.

*   *   *

It is sometimes painful to watch the inhabitants of the political swamp start out pretending to occupy high, dry ground and slowly but surely descend until standards such as "did nothing wrong" are replaced by standards such as "was not convicted" or "was not imprisoned due to the decision being overturned on appeal."

Barney Frank, the gay former congressman from Massachusetts, has at times been an eloquent defender of tolerance of homosexuals. He did the cause of tolerance less service, though, when he was revealed to have a gay prostitution service operating out of his home, as it appears he did from 1985 to 1987. At the beginning of that period, Frank hired gay prostitute Steve Gobie, purportedly employing him as a chauffeur, housekeeper, and assistant as well as paying for Gobie's attorney and court-appointed psychiatrist from prostitution arrests—and using the power of his office to help Gobie fix numerous parking tickets.

Frank claimed to be unaware that Gobie was continuing to run a prostitution service out of Frank's apartment until he was told about it by his landlord, at which point Frank evicted Gobie. Gobie decided that he might be able to make even more money by selling the story of being a politically connected prostitute, leading to a competition between multiple media outlets for the exclusive rights to his story.

Frank invited the House Ethics Committee to investigate him in order to assure that he had done nothing wrong, or at least nothing legally actionable, though it strains credulity to think that Frank had no idea what Gobie was up to, especially given how the two had met. Nonetheless, Congress cleared Frank of involvement in the prostitution ring, he was easily reelected, and the most serious fallout was a 408–18 congressional vote to reprimand Frank for the fixing of the parking tickets.

In classic Washingtonian fashion, the most vocal advocate of expelling Frank from Congress, Representative Larry Craig, Republican of Idaho, had a brush with the law himself after engaging in lewd and lascivious behavior apparently intended to attract sexual attention from a fellow restroom occupant at an airport. The other man in the restroom turned out to be an undercover cop.

There's a pattern of moralizing crusaders in the political realm turning out to be just as dirty if not dirtier than the people they criticize. Take New York's Eliot Spitzer, who presented himself as a crusader not only against Wall Street financial crimes during his two terms as that state's attorney general (prior to becoming its governor) but also against big shot Wall Street traders' frequent hiring of prostitutes. Regardless of what you think about laws against prostitution, you have to agree that Spitzer would be a more credible critic of the profession had he not turned out to be a frequent john himself, notorious forever after as "Client 9," in the FBI reports on the madam whose girls he hired. Adding to Spitzer's embarrassment were reports that he wore black socks during sex, although he denied this. Not a good look for any man but especially not for a prominent politician.

It might have been slightly less embarrassing for Spitzer had the news of his hiring of prostitutes come out while he was still attorney general, with fewer eyes turned toward him. But by the time the world learned of his hypocrisy, he was governor of New York, and his fall from grace was a sight to behold—made all the odder by the fact that the lieutenant governor who rose to fill Spitzer's office was literally unable to see Spitzer, being legally blind. David Paterson was admirably well behaved and soft-spoken during his short two years as governor (not to mention good on some budget issues), which may have been just what the state needed after the tough-talking hypocrite Paterson replaced.

The most fitting part of the whole Eliot Spitzer saga, though, may be that when this purported ethics crusader from Wall Street wanted to engage in liaisons with prostitutes, he headed to D.C.—the Swamp—where scandals are commonplace.

Spitzer's wife, like so many pitiable political wives, stuck with him during the pain of the controversy, only to divorce him five years later, in 2013. Compared to the pressure facing political couples ensnared in criminal investigations, you almost have to see couples torn apart by plain, old-fashioned extramarital affairs as lucky. Emotional conflict is enough to manage without adding crime. And there are plenty of affairs among the denizens of the Swamp. After all, it's not as if they have real work to do, like retail sales or real estate or a thousand other actual jobs.

Another telling example of a badly behaved politician drawn toward the Swamp is Mark Sanford, the former governor of South Carolina. In June of 2009, six years into Sanford's time as governor, it became apparent that for one week neither Sanford's staff nor his wife nor law enforcement knew where he was, though he had told his staff before vanishing that he would be "hiking the Appalachian Trail." When he subsequently failed to respond to numerous cell phone calls, though, and didn't call home on Father's Day, his staff and his wife became concerned.

The mystery was cleared up after a reporter from the South Carolina newspaper *The State* noticed Sanford getting off a plane at the airport—a plane from Argentina. Within hours, realizing that local media were amassing evidence about where he'd really been, Sanford called a press conference and apologized, admitting he had pursued an affair with an Argentine woman (fittingly, one with a degree in international relations) living in Buenos Aires. He later confessed to flirtations with several other women but said he had never "crossed the ultimate line" with them.

The next year, Sanford and his wife divorced (and he resigned his position as head of the Republican Governors Association, but not his governorship), and for years afterward, they remained entangled in custody disputes over their sons and divorce mediation sessions. Sanford wrote extensively about the turmoil on Facebook.

After the ordeal, though, Sanford successfully ran for Congress (where he'd spent three terms before, starting back in the mid-'90s) and moved from South Carolina to D.C. One of the most embarrassingly bungled extramarital affairs in history was not a disqualification from becoming once more a member of Congress, governing his fellow Americans, and rejoining the ecosystem of the Swamp. Bad behavior is almost a badge of membership in the nation's capital.

Sex and power often intermingle. It's certainly not uncommon even in the workplace. The powerful boss takes the young new hire out for cocktails—happens every day. There is a difference, however. These people are paid by the American citizenry. They should be held to a higher, or at least very different, standard. Sex in the Swamp is much more salacious than sex in the workplace for this reason. Call me crazy, but I hold elected officials to a higher standard. After all, I'm paying for their lifestyle.

There is a long history of egregious nonsexual behavior by members of Congress that stretches back to the earliest days of the republic, and we take a look at some of the oldest and most notorious such cases next.

3. BRAWLING IN THE HOUSE

The supreme art of war is to subdue the enemy without fighting.

—SUN TZU

If politicians behave badly in private, in the most shadowy depths of the Swamp, can we at least expect good behavior from them when they're on public display? Can they control themselves on the floor of Congress or in a courtroom?

If the historical record is any indication, no, they cannot.

This shouldn't come as much of a surprise to people watching how volatile today's political figures are. Even the fairly sedate Barack Obama called his Republican opponent Mitt Romney a liar during the 2012 campaign, leading Romney's son Tagg to say he'd like to take a swing at Obama—which then inspired hothead MSNBC commentator Lawrence O'Donnell to taunt Tagg with the on-air remark, "Take a swing at me, and don't worry, there won't be any Secret Service involved. Just us. And I'll make it easy for you. I'll come to you anytime, anywhere. Go ahead, Taggart. Take your best shot."

Most viewers probably took it for a meaningless blast of hot air, but political fistfights do happen. In February 1945, a juncture in history when you'd think American politicians had more important enemies to fight than themselves, two members of the House, both Democrats, got into a fistfight. Representative John E. Rankin of Mississippi called left-wing Representative "Fightin' Frank" Hook (a former boxer) of Michigan a Communist, then became enraged when Hook called him a liar. Rankin grabbed Hook by the neck and punched him several times before other House members separated them. Hook was probably startled to find himself being punched in the face despite his change of careers.

It was a spat on the House floor that nearly led to the first-ever censure by the House of Representatives of one of its own members. That honor almost went to Representative Matthew Lyon of Vermont (he would later serve as a representative from Kentucky as well) back in 1798, a year after he was elected, when he spit on a fellow member of Congress.

Lyon was born near Dublin, Ireland, in 1749 but moved to Connecticut when he was fifteen, later becoming a farmer, father of twelve, and founder of the newspaper *The Scourge of Aristocracy and Repository of Important Political Truth*. He organized a Colonial militia in Vermont during the Revolutionary War, helping to earn him the reputation for leadership that got him elected—though he was also plagued by rumors that desertion during his military service had been punished by making him carry a wooden sword.

Scandal piling upon scandal, in the earliest days of Congress as it is now, Lyon got into a shouting match with another member over whether to expel a man from the Senate. (That senator was William Blount, accused of betraying the United States to the British—but we'll hear more about him, and other foreign entanglements, in the next chapter.) Lyon, a member of the loosely organized Democratic-Republican Party, argued for removal but was met with angry resistance from Federalist Party member Representative Roger Griswold of Connecticut.

Griswold went so far as to condemn Lyon as a "scoundrel," which back in the day meant something in between a fundamentally untrustworthy person and a literal bastard. Lyon proudly defended himself, saying he would fight for what was right and for the good of the people. Griswold made the mistake of mocking Lyon by asking him if he'd fight with his infamous wooden sword.

Being a bastard was one thing, but ridiculing a man's military career was too low a blow. Lyon shot a historic mouthful of tobacco juice at Griswold and went down in history as "the spitting Lyon."

That was on January 30, 1798, but their war was not over yet.

Lyon apologized for breaching the decorum of the House, which he claimed not to realize was in session at the time, and seemed ready to return to business as usual. Griswold, alas, was not satisfied and attacked Lyon, beating him with a cane—on the floor of the House—two weeks later. Lyon was beaten about the head and neck but not yet beaten in spirit. He grabbed fireplace tongs, to the delight of political cartoonists throughout the land, and counterattacked.

The two representatives of their nation scuffled while other members grabbed and dragged them away from each other. A subsequent committee recommended censure for both Lyon and Griswold, but the full House voted against it. Posterity has not quite forgotten, though the example hasn't inspired all of today's politicians to clean up their acts.

One thing the political figures of the early republic have in common with today's is spending a surprising amount of time drunk. Drinking beer was as commonplace as drinking water two centuries ago, even among children. So it should not shock us that one of the first federal judges in U.S. history was impeached in part for being drunk on the bench.

George Washington reportedly wrote instructions to his soldiers, even before the Revolutionary War, telling them, "The foolish and wicked practice of profane cursing and swearing is a vice so mean and low that every person of sense and character detests and despises it."

He should have made the point more forcefully to district court judge John Pickering of New Hampshire, the first U.S. federal official ever removed from his position through impeachment. A Harvard lawyer—at a time when that institution had only a century and a half of experience minting members of the elite—Pickering had previously been appointed to the state superior court of New Hampshire, in 1790, at age fifty-two. The next year, he also was made a member of the American Academy of Arts and Sciences. In retrospect, this period was Pickering's peak.

By 1795, there was already talk at the state level about finding some way to remove him from the bench due to apparent illness that made it difficult for him to focus on his duties. Informal methods for achieving such ends were more common back in those days, too: Even before the Revolution, drunk and angry citizens had been in the habit of forming mobs and chasing corrupt officials (including ones who were themselves drunk) out of town when it appeared necessary. Not all decisions in the eighteenth century were made by lawyers and philosophers.

In one of the fledgling republic's earliest—but by no means last—examples of "failing upward," Pickering was instead appointed by George Washington, to the federal district court for the New Hampshire region, since that entailed a lower workload (actions at the federal level were much rarer in those days, which is usually for the best). By 1800, though, even Pickering's decreased workload could not disguise his increasing distraction and confusion. The court staff wrote to Pickering's superiors, the judges at the First Circuit Court level, but before they could act, a change in the powers of circuit courts in 1802 reduced their influence over district court judges like Pickering, and he stayed on, his reputation notorious as a drunk who rendered bad decisions.

"I shall be sober tomorrow. I am now damned drunk," he famously pronounced at the outset of a hearing in November of that year.

By that time, of course, Pickering had outlasted not only the presidency but the lifetime of George Washington (who left office in 1797 and this mortal plane in 1799), as well as the one-term presidency of John Adams. It fell, then, to the nation's third president, Thomas Jefferson (who had scandals of his own, as you'll recall from the previous chapter), to deal with the Pickering matter. In 1803, Jefferson sent the House evidence of Pickering's illness, intoxication, dubious decisions, and profane remarks. Pickering had abruptly ended one case in his court, suddenly proclaiming that he had "heard enough of the damn'd libels" and could decide the whole case "in four minutes." On another occasion, he agreed to keep listening to witnesses but called them "damn'd scoundrels" (that insult again!) and rejected any witnesses from the government (maybe that part makes sense).

In a fashion that will sound familiar to modern readers, despite the case against Judge Pickering looking pretty strong, the matter became a political football in Congress, where Jefferson's Federalist enemies accused the president of plotting with his fellow Democratic-Republicans to remove a judge (whose mistakes, while embarrassing, were not high crimes and misdemeanors) and thereby threaten the very constitutional order itself. Bad behavior by government officials is not always regarded as a crisis, but trying to *punish* bad behavior by government officials causes an uproar.

One year later, the Senate finally tried Pickering (in absentia) and found him guilty, removing him from office on March 12, 1804, a decade after concerns had first arisen about his capacity to adjudicate. One year after that, at age sixty-seven, Pickering passed away.

★   ★   ★

Jefferson had another political scandal or two brewing much closer to home than New Hampshire, however, in the form of his unruly vice president, Aaron Burr.

Burr remains the only vice president in American history to kill another official of the federal government—namely, the man who, nine years prior to his fatal July 11, 1804, duel with Burr, had been the young nation's first secretary of the treasury, Alexander Hamilton. Hamilton's death was a tragic loss. He was a war hero, a co-writer of the pro-Constitution *Federalist Papers*, a former member of the Continental Congress, founder of the *New York Evening Post*, and creator of a national bank long before he became, in our day, the inspiration for a popular biographical musical—the cast of which gave another vice president, theatergoer Mike Pence, an earful about their liberal political concerns after one performance.

The duel was roughly Hamilton's twelfth, so we should not be surprised by the manner of his death. The duel was also the fourth clash between Burr (a Democratic-Republican, like Jefferson) and Hamilton (a Federalist), though the only one (or possibly the second) of their fights played out with pistols. Once more, scandal had built upon scandal.

In 1791, Burr defeated Hamilton's father-in-law and fellow New Yorker Philip Schuyler in a race for the Senate. Hamilton was not in a forgiving mood that year to begin with, as he was already in the process of becoming the first major political figure in U.S. history involved in a sex scandal, basically paying blackmail money—or paying off a pimp, depending on how you look at it—on a regular basis to a man whose wife Hamilton was sleeping with. That arrangement, like Jefferson's oddly pale slaves, was brought to wider public attention by scandal-loving journalist James Callender.

In 1800—under the presidential election rules of the day—the final choice for president was deadlocked between two Democratic-Republicans with an equal number of electoral votes in the Senate,

Burr and Jefferson. That meant throwing the selection to the House, where Hamilton, though not a member of Congress and not a Democratic-Republican, campaigned tirelessly behind the scenes in favor of Jefferson, simply to avoid making Burr president. He believed Burr to be so untrustworthy that the Federalists would be "signing their own death warrant" if they handed him power. Burr lost the House vote, became vice president instead of president, and would not forgive Hamilton.

In spring 1804, Jefferson dropped Burr from the Federalist presidential ticket, but Hamilton was not yet done harassing Burr. Burr sought as a consolation prize the governorship of New York and had the support of many Federalists, who liked Burr's plan to merge New York with the New England states, then detach that entity from the Union to form a new country, but Hamilton, unlike his fellow Federalists, campaigned for Burr's opponent and spread word of a letter by prominent Democratic-Republican politician and physician Charles Cooper calling Burr a "dangerous" man.

In summer 1804, after a war of letters in which Burr demanded that Hamilton clarify and retract the suggestion by his colleagues that Burr was dangerous, Burr also demanded the opportunity to fight a duel with Hamilton. Hamilton accepted, and the two met in Weehawken, New Jersey.

Although the law in both New Jersey and New York technically prohibited dueling, duels could occur if elaborate enough legal precautions were taken. Some eighteen duels occurred at this same site, in the eighteenth and early nineteenth centuries. New Jersey was a bit more lenient on duelists than New York. Burr and Hamilton were each rowed across the Hudson River in separate boats, their pistols concealed in a carrying case in part so that the rowers could testify later if asked that they had seen no guns. They would keep their backs to Hamilton and Burr during the duel itself, not witnessing the crime in progress.

Hamilton chose—or by lots drawn by the duelists' seconds, received—a position farther north and upstream of Burr. It was traditional for each man in the duel, if he was not actually intent upon killing the other, to fire a symbolic shot at the ground, "throwing away" his shot. Hamilton's and Burr's seconds would later disagree about how much time passed between Hamilton's shot and Burr's, but it appears Hamilton fired first—and fired into the air, well clear of Burr but possibly causing Burr to be confused about Hamilton's intention—and not knowing that Hamilton had vowed before the duel not to merely shoot the ground, too great being Burr's offense in his mind. Instead, he hit a tree well above and behind Burr. Burr fired back, in the direction of Hamilton.

It is unclear whether either man intended to hit the other or simply to fire well clear of his foe—a warning shot being sufficient for the maintenance of honor by the codes of the day, but a shot in self-defense, even a fatal one, being perfectly acceptable from a man being fired upon, if indeed Burr believed Hamilton to be attempting to hit him. In any event, Burr was unharmed and Hamilton was hit in the ribs. In that moment of pain, did Hamilton think Burr had committed one more act of villainy, or had Hamilton known his own shot was fired provocatively? Did he think in a flash of his son Philip (the first of two Hamilton sons so named), killed in a duel three years earlier?

The lead ball Burr fired that day tore apart Hamilton's liver and diaphragm before becoming lodged in his vertebra. Hamilton dropped to the ground in pain immediately, his gun falling from his hand. Burr took a halting step toward Hamilton, in apparent sympathy, but Burr's second, William P. Van Ness, quickly drew Burr away, likely fearing that to linger and see more could create greater legal complications. Van Ness was himself a federal judge, with one brother a former U.S. representative from New York and another brother a future governor of Vermont. He likely realized that the risky business of dueling was turning into an even greater scandal than usual.

The dueling code required the presence of a doctor, and Dr. David Hosack, brought to the site for the occasion, later wrote a letter describing how he heard the two shots but only rushed to see what had happened when his name was called, having intended, like the boatmen, to maintain the plausible deniability of a nonwitness.

Hosack's letter to William Coleman, Hamilton's pick to be the first editor of the *New York Evening Post*, said, "His countenance of death I shall never forget. He had at that instant just strength to say, 'This is a mortal wound, Doctor;' when he sunk away, and became to all appearance lifeless. I immediately stripped up his clothes, and soon, alas I ascertained that the direction of the ball must have been through some vital part." Hosack and Hamilton's second, New York judge Nathaniel Pendleton, carried Hamilton back into his boat and revived him with smelling salts but could do little to mend his terrible injury.

Complicating the account, Hamilton, regaining consciousness, told Hosack that he had not intended to fire and even claimed that his weapon had not yet been fired, suggesting he may not have meant to fire when he did, though most agree his actions were intended to provoke and frighten Burr.

As for Burr, he said after the duel that if his aim had been better, he would have hit Hamilton in the heart.

Within a day, Hamilton died; I can only imagine him lying there in pain and surrounded by family and friends who knew the inevitable was near and that his time on this earth was coming to an end. Burr would soon be charged with murder in both New Jersey and New York, but because the dueling protocols of the day appeared to have been followed, the charges were soon dropped.

The resulting scandal effectively ended Burr's (mainstream) political career, but he traveled west and entertained more dangerous, even secessionist political schemes. We'll revisit the Swamp's capacity for producing disloyalty very soon.

Speaking of secession, one of the heroes of secessionists, Representative John Randolph of Virginia, known for arguing that individual states should be able to nullify the edicts of Washington, was a source of a minor scandal on the House floor a few years after Hamilton's death.

This time it was not so much a battle between man and man as a battle between man and dog. Randolph, a bully racked by tuberculosis pain and opium addiction, owned vicious hunting dogs in addition to some of his fellow human beings. He would bring both to the House floor as a show of strength, intimidating fellow members. The thought of slaves in the capitol building of a country founded (partly) on freedom is perverse by today's standards, but what upset Randolph's fellow members at the time was the dogs.

So intimidating were they that Representative Henry Clay of Kentucky, in 1811 during his first year as Speaker of the House, had to order the dogs removed from the floor. This was a real testament to Clay's will, since no previous Speaker had dared challenge the presence of the dogs.

Other politicians were also hesitant to challenge the angry and violent Randolph, who, like a few other members, was fond of beating people with a cane when challenged. He and Representative Willis Alston of North Carolina reportedly threw plates and silverware at each other at a boardinghouse near the Capitol. They also scuffled on a staircase in the House of Representatives, and Alston must have struck a nerve—like Griswold mocking Lyon's rumored wooden sword—because Randolph proceeded to beat Alston with his cane until Alston bled. Randolph was later fined $20 (equivalent to around $400 today). Both men, of course, resumed making laws for the rest of the populace to obey.

Imagine, if it is even possible, being one of Randolph's slaves instead of an honored colleague in Congress.

The crimes of our politicians have been numerous and varied, but somewhere in between the crime of beating with a cane and shooting someone dead in a duel is the strange case of Representative Robert Potter, another member of the North Carolina delegation to the House.

Potter resigned in 1831, after only two and a half years in Congress and after castrating two men he believed were having affairs with his wife. Incredibly, it wasn't the end of his political career. America believes in second chances. Potter became a North Carolina state legislator—but was later expelled from that legislature for getting into a fight over a game of cards.

All was not yet lost for Potter, though. Having been driven out at both the federal level and the state level in the United States, he was still able to become a legislator (from 1837 to 1841) in another country—a country called Texas, that is, during the decade of its short-lived status as an independent republic broken away from Mexico but not yet a U.S. state.

In early 1842, amid fighting between rival factions of Texas landowners called the Regulators and Moderators (who fought a small war despite their reassuring-sounding names), Potter was shot when his home was surrounded by Regulators, and he fell into a nearby lake and drowned.

A novel partly based on his life and death bears the poetic title *Love Is a Wild Assault*.

The next decade saw a return to good old-fashioned cane beating in Congress. Before this time, numerous political figures had beaten others with canes over the course of early U.S. history—such as former Tennessee governor Sam Houston, who gave Representative

William Stanbery of Ohio a thumping on the streets of D.C. after a Stanbery speech on the House floor accusing Houston of giving out fraudulent rations contracts. But canes were by no means the only weapons used by politicians during that period; Andrew Jackson had absorbed a couple of shots, one to an artery that nearly killed him, during a street fight with a rival military man before becoming president.

Combining different forms of weaponry, in 1856, a pro-slavery South Carolina congressman, Preston Brooks, severely beat abolitionist Massachusetts senator Charles Sumner with his cane while two of Brooks's allies held off other senators at gunpoint. (That must have been against Senate decorum rules, even in the nineteenth century.) The incident is sometimes seen as a tiny precursor to the impending Civil War.

Not to be outdone, ten years later, after the war and the restoration of civility, Representative Lovell H. Rousseau of Kentucky beat Representative Josiah B. Grinnell of Iowa with an iron-handled cane until it broke. Like Brooks, Rousseau was aided by armed supporters, who kept other members of the House from intervening to help Grinnell. Much like Lyon, Rousseau had finally snapped after repeated verbal arguments with his victim when his war record was impugned—though this time the Civil War was the conflict in question.

Given all the nation had just been through, it's remarkable that men from both the North and South were serving in the same legislature, and usually not beating each other senseless— but Rousseau and Grinnell did not have the excuse of regional differences. Both were Union men, and Rousseau insisted that despite being from Kentucky, he had commanded regiments from Iowa under fire during the war, a claim that Iowan Grinnell mocked three days before his June 14, 1866, beating.

After the beating, an investigatory committee recommended

censuring both men, Grinnell for the personal mockery and Rousseau for the beating, but Grinnell was cleared on July 16 and Rousseau censured, though not expelled, on July 21. Rousseau resigned in protest later that same day—but in the resulting special election called in Kentucky, his adoring constituents sent him back to Congress. There he completed his term, and he and Grinnell both exited Congress in 1867, after the next regular election.

Enmity between states also couldn't really be blamed for two senators being censured in 1902 for a fistfight in the Senate. Benjamin R. Tillman and John McLaurin were both Democrats of South Carolina, McLaurin the junior and angry because Tillman accused him of corruption and being led by "improper influences." McLaurin shouted that Tillman was engaging in "a willful, malicious, and deliberate lie," at which point Tillman ran across the chamber and punched McLaurin. However, it was Tillman who ended up with a bloody nose, and the rarely deployed sergeant at arms of the Senate, along with some helpful senators, had to break up the fight.

In theory, the Progressive Era was meant to put an end to the kinds of graft Tillman was alleging, but his fistfight in the Senate, taking place early in the presidency of the first of the two Progressive giants, Teddy Roosevelt and Woodrow Wilson, is a reminder that nothing in the Swamp is ever completely clean or rational.

It's true, of course, that the floors of some other legislative chambers around the world are more prone than our own to violence (see: Ukraine, Japan, South Africa, etc.) or name-calling (see: England). But maybe that's one more reason to worry about numerous Swamp creatures who have devoted themselves to trying to sell out American interests to foreign powers, something President Trump has recently warned us about—and something that, as we shall see, has been going on since before the United States was even a country.

* * *

It's at this point I should be fully honest. I am no stranger to the fistfight. In fact, I have been involved in my fair share. Being from a rough inner-city neighborhood in Chicago, sometimes there was no other way to resolve a conflict. One night, when walking back to my car, I was confronted by a group of guys, maybe five or so. After denying them their request (my wallet), I found myself getting hit from all directions with fists. I tried to defend myself as best I could (my dad would later pat me on the back for my effort), but I eventually found shelter along the curb, guarding my head and taking kicks as well. Oh, and they took my wallet.

Or there's the time I defended myself against a couple of bullies on the Chicago trading floor, where I started my business career. It was a rough-and-tumble place, the energy trading area where literally hundreds of men would stand in a pit and trade money versus oil. For every dollar earned, there was a dollar lost by someone in that pit, so fights were routine. Mix emotion with money, then add tight quarters—and splash that environment with testosterone—and, well, you get the picture. I spent more than a few days off in suspension for fighting, and thousands of dollars in decorum fines.

I'm just trying to explain that while I am no stranger to the fistfight, I am a private citizen and not an elected official. There is a difference, and that should be noted.

4. FOREIGN ENTANGLEMENTS

Peace, commerce, and honest friendship with all nations—entangling alliances with none.

—THOMAS JEFFERSON

It's bad enough when the Swamp creatures care more about their own fights and conflicts than they do about the rest of the country—but what about when they take the side of some other country against the United States? It's not just something that went on during the Cold War days of spy versus spy. Accusations of such activity have been common since the United States was born.

Even before the Revolutionary War was over, a U.S. diplomat assigned to France was accused of treason.

The fall from grace of diplomat Silas Deane began with charges of financial impropriety. In the summer of 1778, the first U.S. diplomat to France was probably feeling melancholy but unafraid as he sailed westward across the Atlantic, back home to the rebelling United States, summoned to report to the Continental Congress in Philadelphia. Sailing on the same ship, seemingly held in the same high regard, was the very first official French ambassador to the new American nation.

Deane, a Connecticut lawyer before becoming a member of the

Continental Congress and then envoy to France, had received news in 1777, while in France, of his wife's passing away. He likely did not expect his return to bring a new personal crisis, but upon his return to Philadelphia on July 14, 1778, he was first accused of skimming from his budget for supplies from France to the Colonial military. Not having brought his accounting records with him from France, he was hard-pressed by accusations from his fellow envoy Arthur Lee—though robustly defended by famed Continental Congress delegate from New York (and future first-ever secretary of state) John Jay.

For Deane to be accused of financial impropriety at any point in time would be damaging, but to be so accused at a time when the United States had only just become a country and was fighting for its life was tantamount to calling someone a heretic in the midst of a sacred struggle. The United States desperately needed France's aid if it was going to survive a fight with the British Empire, and few scandalous whiffs could smell ranker than an accusation of exploiting the France-U.S. alliance for personal gain. In a world still dominated by monarchies, France and the United States were for a short time seen as republican siblings making common cause for a better world. It would be the gravest embarrassment if Deane were deemed an old-fashioned thief.

In typical eighteenth-century style, the battle was partly fought in the media of the day, in such forms as Deane's lengthy newspaper essay "The Address of Silas Deane to the Free and Virtuous Citizens of America." Inauspiciously, during the debate, Deane stayed with his fellow Connecticuter Benedict Arnold. Eventually, the Continental Congress offered to give more money to Deane to compensate him for many expenses he had already incurred in arranging shipments to the United States, but they also wanted him to finalize his dealings with France, collect his records, and return home for good.

Word that he was at odds with the Continental Congress reached England's King George III, and there were plans in George's court to try bribing Deane into betraying the American cause. The British decided it wasn't worth their while to bribe him, though, when they intercepted letters of Deane's in which he said he was already despairing of the United States being able to beat the British and was considering urging the Continental Congress to negotiate a peaceful compromise. It does not appear that Deane intended to harm the United States or to have his correspondence be made public, but it was published in a Tory newspaper in British-held New York City, and Deane, already plagued by a cloud of suspicion over the financial squabble, was now seen as a traitor to the American cause.

For the rest of the 1780s, Deane lived in what is now Belgium, planning to rebuild his personal fortune and restore his reputation, but illness and further financial turmoil ended with his death in 1789 as he awaited his ship's departure for America.

Twenty-first-century Americans—if they remember history at all—probably forget that hostility between the United States and England did not end when the Revolutionary War concluded in 1783.

Fourteen years after the war, in 1797, a senator was expelled for trying to help the British take over part of Florida. That man was William Blount of Tennessee, who you'll recall from the last chapter as inspiring the arguments that led to Representative Matthew Lyon spitting on Representative Roger Griswold.

Inspiring a spit fight was hardly Blount's worst crime. He remains one of only four men in history expelled from the Senate, and the only one ousted for a reason other than the Civil War.

Blount conspired with others to get the Creek and Cherokee tribes to lend fighting men to the British to aid them in conquering the territory of West Florida, which was then in Spanish hands

(Spain, remember, had colonies well before the English did). Blount was convinced that the West was the United States' true destiny, and if nothing else, he was certain that the vast tracts of land he and his brothers held out west would only increase in value if the United States or its allies, not Spain or a politically unstable France, retained the right to own land out there.

Blount had been a Continental Congressman from North Carolina, where he was active in promoting the new Constitution, and Speaker of the Senate in Tennessee. In the early 1790s, during his tenure as governor of the Southwest Territory, though—and during his ill-fated subsequent one year as a U.S. senator from Tennessee—he began concocting a plan aimed simultaneously at protecting the United States and (perhaps more important) shoring up the plummeting value of the vast tracts of land he and his brothers had bought west of the Mississippi.

With U.S. citizens' holdings already declining in value out west, Blount and others were terrified that territory held by the Spanish was ripe for conquest by France, which by 1795 had defeated Spain in the War of the Pyrenees and might next seize all lands held by Americans in the vast Louisiana Territory. Blount hoped to resolve a complex situation already involving three nations by introducing a fourth into the equation.

If Britain, still smarting from the loss of its own New World colonies, could be induced to seize the Spanish territory before France did, Britain might be more amenable to guaranteeing U.S. merchants access to the Mississippi and points beyond, preventing the complete collapse of investments in western lands, including the Blounts'. Getting some Native Americans to fight alongside the British on the basis of the usual false promises about returning ancestral lands to them could sweeten the deal. Blount had become accustomed to deploying troops and making deals without consulting Congress in his capacity as governor of the Southwest Territory, now Tennessee. Sending some of his Creek and Cherokee allies to New Orleans to help secure it for the British was in that sense an extension of his usual maverick policy-making.

His plan just happened to have the consequence, if it worked, of stabilizing control of the West and immediately jacking up the Blount brothers' faltering land prices. His brothers knew that, but there was no reason the public or Congress need dwell on it.

It was no stranger a scheme than some of the official alliances made by governments at the time, but unauthorized plans for co-ordinating military alliances on the North American continent were frowned upon then, as they are now. Spies got their hands on a letter of Blount's outlining the entire scheme and turned it over to the United States' third secretary of state, Timothy Pickering, who had long been suspicious of Blount and seized upon the opportunity to attack him. Pickering turned the letter over to then-president John Adams, who in turn sent the letter to be read on July 3, 1797, to the Senate, then located in Philadelphia. It was duly read, at a time when Senator Blount was out for a walk.

They read it again when he returned, and he was not happy. Within days, Blount countered with a letter to the Senate defending himself, then with testimony before an investigatory committee, but, consulting with his lawyers, he ultimately decided to skip bail—while his Senate seat was "sequestered" pending further investigation—and head back to Tennessee.

In familiar political fashion, the case became another partisan melee, with the Federalists condemning Blount and his fellow Democratic-Republicans defending him. Worse for Blount, George Washington himself weighed in, saying Blount deserved the "de-testation of all good men." President Adams's wife, Abigail, said Blount deserved the guillotine. Secretary of State Pickering, for his part, suspected a much wider plot and accused Jefferson of being behind it.

*   *   *

At roughly the same time, Brigadier General James Wilkinson, later governor of part of the Louisiana Purchase, conspired with the country on the other side of Blount's hoped-for British–Spanish conflict: Wilkinson hoped to get Kentucky to secede and join the Spanish territories. Wilkinson is arguably the greatest villain in American history, and we'll see that he time and again conspired against the United States.

Wilkinson's superior, General Anthony Wayne, intercepted Spanish spies carrying money to Wilkinson—whom Wayne already hated because of Wilkinson's frequent attempts to undermine Wayne and curry favor with George Washington. Wilkinson was providing information to the Spanish about the activities of both the French and British in the Southeast. Yet Wilkinson escaped the law's grasp on this occasion because his longtime enemy Wayne died of a stomach ulcer in 1796. With his chief accuser out of the way, Wilkinson ascended to the position of senior officer of the army.

Helping to take control of the Louisiana Purchase in 1803, which had been bought by Jefferson during his first term as president, Wilkinson secretly maintained his contacts with Spain, even giving that nation advice on how to contain booming U.S. territorial expansion. That's right: One of the men in charge of the largest new piece of American territory up to that time was also working behind the scenes to restrict America's growth. If our manifest destiny was to expand across the continent, the name *Wilkinson* should go down in U.S. history as one as vilified as *Benedict Arnold*.

And still Wilkinson's treasonous activities were not over. He would conspire against the U.S. government with another recurring villain in our story, Aaron Burr. Burr, whom we met in the previous chapter as a vice president turned dueling killer of Alexander Hamilton, next attempted to turn part of the Louisiana Purchase into his own country—possibly one extending all the way to the

modern Southwest and into Mexico, or if Burr is to be believed, merely a large and innocent farm plot in Texas. For this, he would eventually be arrested but acquitted. Starting your own country is certainly one way to decrease the odds of having to take orders from presidents or former secretaries of the treasury you dislike.

Burr's plot was outlined in a coded letter to Wilkinson that historians call "the Cipher Letter," though Burr denied having written it. It is very unlikely that Wilkinson himself wrote it—but he did *edit* it, removing parts that incriminated him and trying to make Burr sound like the sole mastermind. It appears that several large landowners west of the Mississippi were involved, along with several military men and a territorial governor or two.

Burr was arrested on Jefferson's orders, escaped custody and fled into the wilderness of the Mississippi Territory, was arrested again in 1807, and eventually was acquitted at trial in Virginia. After that, he moved to Europe and made a similar attempt to found his own nation by pleading with the British to let him foment a revolution in Mexico. The British were unpersuaded, and in 1811, Burr returned to the United States, changed his name to Edwards, resumed his old law practice, and remarried and divorced before dying in 1836.

Wilkinson had by then died in Mexico, as it happens, in 1825, after military commands in Canada and New Orleans territories—but not before two more investigations into his western land plotting, including an 1811 court-martial investigation ordered by then–president James Madison.

We remember history's patriots, but the fledgling United States was a fragile construction with shifting boundaries, shifting loyalties, and some shady characters. At least the physical boundaries are a bit clearer today. National loyalties? They're still in flux.

One of the ways in which the Founding Era resonates with our own is that the very definition of *nation* was in flux—and that ambiguity

offered a lot of opportunities for bad behavior. Did a country have to be made up entirely of contiguous land? Could foreigners buy land here on the same terms as U.S. citizens? What should be the rules for claiming previously unowned land? (And what was to become of Native American tribes if European settlers stubbornly refused to recognize their ancestral territories as property rights?)

For most of the twentieth century, by contrast—since the admission of Arizona as the forty-eighth state in 1912—the United States had usually seen itself as one intact, almost naturally occurring political entity, stretching from sea to sea and forging a single people from all the teeming masses within, however many difficulties they might from time to time create for each other.

However, one of the important themes President Donald Trump tapped into in his history-making election campaign of 2016, and continued to sound once in office, was that the inhabitants of the D.C. Swamp don't necessarily think in the same nationalist terms that the average American does. It's not as simple, however, as saying that the D.C. crowd is too left-wing for right-wing citizens. It's not just a matter of the federal government having alliances with and allegiances to governments overseas. Nor an issue of "transnational" corporations caring more about the bottom line than about the inhabitants of any one land.

After all, we *want* the United States to be friendly with other governments if the alternative is war. We want U.S. companies to export goods to other nations. But while the average American still lives his or her life in a single state and may not even own a passport, the elite have become so accustomed to working with, traveling with, communicating with, and, more worryingly, governing with their elite counterparts in other nations, it becomes unclear whether they remain, at heart, Americans first.

Again, this is in itself no crime. America has outgrown explicit loyalty oaths, at least for people who were born here. But it should

give us pause if the elites who govern Americans are not as loyal to their countrymen as they are to the rising institutions of global governance that emerged in the twentieth century, such as the United Nations or the European Union—institutions that have come to be distrusted by many people within and beyond the United States in the twenty-first century.

The fact that Americans take pride in their country has long been viewed as a bit of an embarrassment by the global elite, something Trump tapped into with small but meaningful gestures as simple as his red "Make America Great Again" hat. He knew intuitively, even when his ideological opponents thought they had all the statistics and expertise on their side, that regular Americans resented being told that there was nothing they could do in the face of the great globalist tide that was robbing them of their livelihood. Americans don't like being told that their loyalty to country, their patriotism, is retrograde or hateful.

They know the broad strokes of the American vision are good and humane even when they must quietly submit to lecturing by elitists who claim to know all the details better—but who may be paying more attention to some big-picture and questionable statistics than to the local factory being relocated overseas, to young people coming back maimed from protracted overseas conflicts of dubious value for keeping America safe, or to crime victims asking why (some) illegal aliens keep being deported after committing assaults or thefts only to simply turn around and walk across the border again.

The period of globalism that came to full flower after the Cold War ended in 1989 has seen great economic opportunity and, despite the 2008 financial crisis and other setbacks, a rising tide of prosperity around the world by any reasonable historical measure. Yet it has also seen an erosion of national sovereignty. It's not just a "retrograde" American impulse. Europeans, too, have begun to realize that as much as they might dislike their own national politicians, they have far more control over those politicians than they do over the cold-blooded bureaucracy of the EU and the detached, haughty European Parliament.

When push comes to shove, will elite politicians and bureaucrats who, say, live in D.C., summer in France, and lobby for small but rich island nations on the other side of the world have our backs? As a billionaire businessman, Trump got to know them well, and he suspects the answer is no. If nothing else, it's very hard to keep an eye on bureaucracies responsible for people in distant nations if you can barely figure out what's going on in the Swamp close to home.

In the United States, we don't see the machinations of the European Parliament up close and personal—but right here in the town where I work, New York City, we can see another of the biggest, most wasteful international bureaucracies in human history at work: the United Nations.

There were howls of outrage from the creatures of the Swamp when Trump, mere weeks after being elected—at a time when some people assumed he should be trying to "tone it down" and look like all the other politicians—tweeted that the much-praised United Nations is really "just a club for people to get together, talk, and have a good time. So sad!" He had earlier tweeted, ominously in the minds of some, "As to the UN, things will be different after Jan. 20th," his inauguration day.

Of course, there's at least one other thing the United Nations does, which is constantly pass, or attempt to pass, resolutions condemning U.S. ally Israel. With 193 member countries, about a quarter of them Muslim-majority countries, and each getting one vote, the United Nations proposes a steady stream of anti-Israel resolutions even when it doesn't do much else to speak of. (The United States'

Security Council veto power has usually been crucial in derailing such resolutions, which have no real binding power anyway, but the Obama administration, as if long champing at the bit, seized the opportunity to change that pattern in its final days, after the 2016 election, encouraging one last anti-Israel resolution that the United States would not block, which condemned Israeli settlement construction.)

Regardless of its political leanings, though, the United Nations definitely does one thing that should bother Americans and frugal people the world over: It wastes a hell of a lot of money. Its annual budget is about $5 billion—and about $3 billion of that comes from U.S. taxpayers alone, about $1 billion as annual dues and another $2 billion for various ongoing UN projects. What are we getting for our money? Not the loyalty of the globe, apparently, and not love for our main Middle Eastern ally.

Trump's temptation to stop paying the United States' massive dues, and disentangle us from the ultimate foreign alliance in the process, is heresy to the global elite who feel more like "citizens of the world" than like Americans (or Frenchmen or Chinese or Germans, and so on). But even with a few truly noble projects to its credit—like getting rid of potentially dangerous land mines left behind by long-ago wars all over the world—how does the UN prioritize its spending? The real scandal is that UN bureaucrats prioritize pretty much the same way D.C. politicians do: They think of their own needs first.

Although it might take only a few million dollars to save kids from starvation, prevent infectious disease, or protect the world's poorest from extreme cases of air pollution, the UN is slated to spend billions this decade—on refurbishing its own lavish headquarters on the east side of Manhattan. Just a couple of blocks north is a newer tower, the Trump World Tower complex, companion to the now-famous Trump Tower in Midtown Manhattan.

The Trump World Tower was built at a cost of about $300 million of private money, and obviously, its owner hopes to earn that much and more from using and renting the place. The United Nations refurbishing has cost some $2 billion, and the UN wants at least $3 billion more for additional New York facilities and refurbished offices in Geneva—much of that at U.S. taxpayer expense, remember.

Maybe UN staff would have more money with which to pay their own bills if they weren't hiring large numbers of New York City prostitutes, buying fancy cars with which they career recklessly through East Side Manhattan streets knowing diplomatic immunity will get them out of most traffic violations, and taking helicopter rides to conferences on philanthropic-sounding but largely useless topics like fostering global harmony or sharing our common humanness. The United States pays many of their official bills, and about all we get for it is condescending lectures and traffic congestion.

Do we really think the delegates and bureaucrats who discuss the fate of the world at these facilities burn with an urgent desire to get money to those most in need out in the most troubled spots in the world? Most of them probably burn with an urgent desire to try out new East Side bars and restaurants. And when they get done with that and finally have to head home to their own countries, most will support the kinds of socialist policies and big-government spending projects that made the world's poor so poor in the first place. Then, to compound the problem, the delegates sometimes deploy UN peacekeeping troops who commit crimes of their own—rape, bribe-taking, theft.

One of the UN peacekeepers' favorite crimes is sexual exploitation of the locals where they're keeping the peace. As *Newsweek* reported, "While no UN mission was immune, [an internal UN report about the problem] singled out as egregious four missions in

Haiti, the Democratic Republic of Congo, Liberia, and Sudan/ South Sudan. Moreover, the report suggested a disturbing trend: In 36 percent of cases, the alleged victims were minors."

Even the liberal *New Republic* magazine, observing debates over the UN budget back in the 1980s, opined, "Let It Sink."

At the moment, though, that attitude is heresy to the international elitists. While the UN holds ceremonies to honor the late dictator and mass murderer Fidel Castro as a hero to the world's poor, the organization routinely criticizes the United States for its "structural racism" and gun culture—all the while doling out subsidies (funded by our own money) for cities that make efforts to move away from car culture toward the mass transit and pedestrian activity the UN considers more futuristic and forward-looking.

The UN symbolizes the elite's ideal of a single, harmonious, moral world with them in charge—while in reality, it gives them more opportunities to crawl out of their local swamps and create scandals that slime the whole planet. President Obama apparently approved, upping the United States' contribution to the UN by about 50 percent over the course of his presidency, including $9.2 billion just as he was exiting the White House. One of the Trump administration's first acts was to freeze an additional $221 million payment to the UN's good friends, the Palestinian Authority.

After all, despite that old saying about patriotism being the last refuge of scoundrels, huge international bureaucracies provide badly behaved people with plenty of places to hide.

5. LOBBYING IN THE SWAMP

Greed is a bottomless pit which exhausts the person in an endless effort to satisfy the need without ever reaching satisfaction.

—ERICH FROMM

There is nothing—I repeat, *nothing*—that ticks me off more than the corruption, cronyism, and greedy Swamp behavior involving lobbyists.

Huge sums of money are traded for access to and persuasion of our elected officials. The more power the elected official has, the more money made available to him or her from an endless well of funds. Corporations seek deals or regulation rollbacks. Foreign governments seek access to our markets and, therefore, every American consumer's wallet. And sometimes, it's just sheer greed by Swamp dwellers to acquire more and more of the power or money or fame that drives lawmakers to vote in the way that most enriches them instead of voting for the right thing.

Lobbyists are the brokers of the influence-for-sale transactions that have become commonplace in D.C. Go to any fine restaurant or popular bar around town and you'll most definitely see a congressman or senator or staffer being wined and dined. The lobbyist at the table is the one who aggressively reaches for the substantial tab at the end of the expensive meal.

Obviously, government, which is simply a small group of people who have control over everyone else's money, will create lots of opportunities for unscrupulous people to get rich.

This is not a new development. Nearly two centuries ago, one of President Andrew Jackson's customs officials, Samuel Swartwout, skimmed $1,225,705.69 (about $30 million in today's money) from his two terms as collector of customs in the trade-filled and lucrative port city of New York, then fled to London, according to testimony delivered to Congress in 1839, a few years after Jackson, who had been an ally of Swartwout, was out of the White House. It wasn't hard for Swartwout to find large amounts of money to skim. New York's customs fees accounted for over half the funds in the U.S. Treasury in those days.

Swartwout was only allowed to return to the United States if he agreed to a compromise whereby he returned a portion of the money. It may sound shocking that he didn't end up in jail, but in those days, it was largely taken for granted that customs agents would keep some of the money they collected, in much the same way tax collectors were incentivized in still earlier times by the right to keep some of what they squeezed out of the citizens. Swartwout lived as a free man until his death in 1856.

But then, as the old joke goes, *the real crime is what's legal.* Private citizens aren't supposed to just walk up to the U.S. Treasury and grab handfuls of cash, but in our own day, they can butter up and spoil politicians to get them to pour some legal cash into certain select citizens' troughs. That buttering up is the essence of the lobbying business, and it should be no surprise it regularly results in scandals.

Senator Alan Cranston of California and four other senators were reprimanded in 1990 for meeting with the head of the Federal Home

Loan Bank Board's San Francisco branch about helping out the faltering savings and loan run by Charles H. Keating Jr., who had contributed to their campaigns.

Two members of the House were indicted and three reprimanded in 1976 for taking gifts from South Korean agent Tongsun Park (a scandal nicknamed "Koreagate").

Back in 1962, Bobby Baker, secretary to the Senate majority leader, organized the Serv-U Corporation to sell vending machines to companies seeking federal grants. This led to an investigation of his networking activities within the Senate, such as introducing lobbyists to members of Congress—and accusations that he provided prostitutes to members who voted as he wanted them to and who made deals with government contractors of his choosing. Baker ended up being convicted of tax evasion and doing eighteen months in prison.

Such conflicts of interest have arisen for centuries, though. In 1872, America learned that the Crédit Mobilier construction company, which was working on the Union Pacific railroad and wanted to smooth its approval by Congress, had provided multiple members of the House, four senators, the secretary of the treasury, and even Vice President Schuyler Colfax with cash and millions of dollars' worth of discounted stock. The scandal was seen as emblematic of the corruption of the Gilded Age—but it didn't stop one of the stock recipients, Representative James Garfield of Ohio, from going on to be elected president eight years later.

Given that a few million dollars' worth of wining and dining or exotic travel junkets could determine the fate of billions of dollars of taxpayer money, it's surprising there isn't even more money sloshing around the lobbying grotto of the Swamp.

One recent scandal in that dark corner of the Swamp revolves around the late pharmaceutical lobbyist Evan Morris. As *The Wall*

Street Journal's Brody Mullins reports, Morris's work on behalf of Swiss pharma giant Roche led to him commanding a budget of about $50 million a year, paying hundreds of lobbyists and consultants: "His apparent success afforded luxuries including $2,000 bottles of wine, a $3 million waterfront vacation home, a $300,000 mahogany speedboat and four Porsches. He belonged to eight private golf courses and hired top chefs to cook for dinner parties at his home."

Now Morris is suspected by government investigators of embezzling millions of dollars via kickbacks from consultants who were being paid by Roche—and investigators think a wide array of Swamp creatures, including media strategists, consultants, political advisors, and other lobbyists like him, may have helped him conceal his activities.

"Prosecutors are investigating whether Mr. Morris took company money to pay for real estate, golf memberships, Rolex watches, fancy wine, and cigars," writes Mullins. "Among Washington lobbyists, Mr. Morris was an early pioneer in the practice of exploiting gaps in disclosure laws for companies to spend millions of dollars, much of it untraceable, to fund stealthy influence campaigns."

Those influence campaigns sometimes resembled what have long been called "AstroTurf" operations—throwing money at a policy cause covertly to make it appear there has been a sudden upsurge in grassroots interest among the public. Mullins called the practice "black ops" spending, as though he were an intelligence agency.

Prior to working directly for Roche, Morris was employed by the lobbying firm Patton Boggs, which did work on behalf of Roche—and which has strong ties to the Democratic Party, as did Morris, having been a White House intern in the Bill Clinton years. The incestuous connections between companies, lobbyists, lawyers, and politicians ensure that when a crisis arises that calls for some response, the well connected are ready to steer that response in a direction that just happens to help their clients. In the George W. Bush years, Morris was instrumental in turning an avian flu scare into an opportunity for Roche to sell vast emergency supplies of Tamiflu pills as the (taxpayer-funded) solution, at a price of $1 billion. Morris also worked his magic to ensure the FDA allowed sales of the breast cancer drug Avastin, though its efficacy continued to be debated.

With everyone around him telling him he was a star responsible for raking in millions, maybe it's not surprising that Morris, a bit like Andrew Jackson's New York customs collector, may have decided he was entitled to a little extra. Whether with ill-gotten or standard gains, Morris in the mid-2000s bought a Porsche, moved into a $1.7 million house in a Virginia suburb, told neighbors he spent another million on renovations, and created a wine cellar at home and a collection of a thousand cigars at his office at Roche-affiliated Genentech in D.C. Mullins also reports that a former colleague of Morris recalls his ordering a $2,000 bottle of wine at lunch.

But it's not the goodies—or the fact that Morris started to tell what seemed to be contradictory stories about how he paid for them (including claiming the Clinton Foundation covered his multiple country club memberships)—that threaten to drag the American government down into the Swamp. It's the fact that shady characters such as Morris routinely command vast lobbying budgets and the ability to coordinate political donations.

Roche and Genentech employees donated more than $1 million to both the Republican and Democratic Governors Associations. But there are many other ways lobbyists can exert influence without directly talking to members of Congress about their policy preferences, like the nearly $400,000 Morris steered toward the Clinton Foundation from Roche and Genentech, the fund-raising event at a golf course he organized for a Democratic legislator, or the $750,000 Genentech donated to Obama inauguration festivities.

Unfortunately for Morris, a random audit suggested that he was submitting expense reports for events and lobbying activities that had never existed, in addition to all the big-ticket ones that did.

When an internal Genentech investigation led to lawyers calling Morris for a long-overdue talk, he was planning on doing one last big fund-raiser for Hillary and then trying to secure an ambassadorship to Switzerland. Instead, he ducked out of a meeting with inquisitive Genentech executives, began avoiding phone calls even from his wife, purchased a gun, and after a relaxing drink at a Virginia golf club, shot himself.

I love the free market, but that *doesn't* mean I defend what businesses do once they see how much money they can make by sucking at the government teat instead of making goods and services for ordinary customers. While we argue about the merits of the market versus government programs, the Swamp creatures in D.C. are most at home in the mushy area where the two meet. Once large amounts of money start changing hands, people tend to stop caring whether the money came from U.S. companies, U.S. government programs, foreign companies, or foreign government programs. The harder it is to tell, the more the networkers and dealmakers of the Swamp tend to thrive.

Since Trump's election, the media have been obsessed with his ties to Russia. Curiously, they do not seem alarmed by the even stronger and more lucrative ties of numerous major Democratic donors to Russia, as Hoover Institution fellow Paul Roderick Gregory observes on Forbes.com.

The Podesta Group (founded by the brother of Hillary Clinton's campaign chairman) lobbied for Russia's largest bank, Sberbank, which is directly tied to the Kremlin, according to intelligence officials. Tony Podesta also received about $900,000 from a group that lobbied on behalf of Viktor Yanukovych, the ousted Putin-allied

Ukrainian president. The Podesta Group also successfully lobbied their pal Hillary Clinton, while she was secretary of state, to let a Russian company, whose chairman made a big donation to the Clinton Foundation, buy about a fifth of the U.S. uranium supply. A Russian bank affiliated with the company paid Bill Clinton a half million dollars just before the deal went through.

Should we be alarmed that the Democrats are so cozy with Russia? If so, that doesn't seem to be the narrative from the mainstream media lately. Yet minor Russian ties to Trump people are supposed to show he's a "Manchurian candidate" manipulated by foreign powers. It's always scary when Trump does it, I guess.

"Lobbying for Russia is a bi-partisan activity," writes Gregory. "No wonder that Trump's 'drain the swamp' and anti-media messages resonate so well with mainstream America."

But how does one go about actually limiting the kinds of activities, the influence-peddling and special-interest legislation, that the Swamp facilitates? It's not easy, because every time the rules of conduct change to prevent graft, the Swamp creatures and their lawyers get to work on finding new ways around the rules, or slimier ways to evade the spirit of the rules.

Former lobbyist Jack Abramoff was, by his own admission, "arrogant" early in his political career, directing a grassroots lobby associated with the Reagan White House, but when he failed to get along with Chief of Staff Donald Regan, he left to work in movie production for ten years (he conceived and produced the Dolph Lundgren anticommunist action film *Red Scorpion*) and then became a lobbyist. It was a noble calling in his mind, and he fought for free-market causes he believed in, such as keeping regulators' hands off Microsoft. Due to his political successes, though, he began to think, like many lobbyists, that "the rules didn't apply to him," and, as he recounted to me in early 2017, he pled guilty to charges that stemmed from 2000 scheme involving faking a wire transfer of money to encourage other investors to join a casino-buying effort, and went to prison for three and a half years over lobbying violations.

He devoted some of his time after he got out of prison to writing and speaking about how hard it really is to craft effective anticorruption rules, at least when there are smart lobbyists like him around. For example, congressional staffers moonlight for companies while they're working in the offices of members of Congress.

But as Abramoff explains, there isn't much the law can do to prevent a company executive who talks to a young, financially needy congressional staffer from heavily hinting that he likes the quality of a staffer's work and maybe the staffer should come work for the exec in a high paying job someday after leaving Congress. It's not an immediate, tangible bribe, but it can work almost like a down payment on one. It may at least create excitement and interest in the mind of the young and possibly overworked staffer. Suddenly, the staffer associates the company with better days ahead, and even if that subsequent job is never taken, the staffer may be ever so slightly more sympathetic to legislation that gives that company a more-than-fair shake.

Abramoff says the practical limit on that tactic is just the fact that you have to have a pretty big firm to ensure that you can keep making good on the jobs you offer people.

The last time Congress made any serious attempt at reforming the rules about lobbying was a decade ago. The new rules were "replete with loopholes," Abramoff told me, and "people have found their way through the loopholes." He says most lobbying-related corruption is nearly impossible to police because a central corrupt activity will be concealed within a veneer of propriety, the underlying motives hard to prove, as when a politician is not bribed outright but the politician's spouse is given a cushy job by the organization doing the lobbying.

If they insist the spouse was the best person for the job, how likely is the public to notice and argue otherwise?

Furthermore, warns Abramoff, the main thing giving the lobbyist (and the special interests for whom the lobbyist works) an unfair advantage over his fellow citizens is not always tangible gifts or envelopes of cash slipped to a senator. The lobbyist's most precious resource is time—time in proximity to the politicians he is out to influence.

The average citizen might glimpse a prominent politician for just a few seconds during a parade, maybe shake his hand. The lobbyist specializes in setting up events such as golf games and fund-raising dinners—"any amount of meals, any amount of golf" under the current rules, says Abramoff—that give his clients plenty of time in direct contact with the politician who needs to be influenced.

He organized campaign contributions, dinners, and use of his plane, Abramoff told me. He could offer his clients "golf trips to Scotland with congressmen." Time traveling together with politicians gives lobbyists and their clients "the keys to the kingdom," he says.

Furthermore, the lobbyist is not out just to trick or bribe. "The essence of a lobbyist is access and *persuasion*," says Abramoff, still with some palpable respect for his old art form. It's a skill.

What can be done to limit the use of those skills for nefarious ends in D.C., though? I asked Abramoff if Trump, who emphasized during his presidential campaign that he understands the process of influence peddling, can do anything to rein in the lobbying culture.

"All the corruption on Capitol Hill is controlled by Congress," Abramoff cautioned, "not by the administration." Congress, he thinks, will always resist serious attempts to reform that culture of corruption because he estimates 80 percent of the benefits of holding their jobs comes from the direct or incidental influence upon them of lobbying industries and pressure groups. Government is work, at least some of the time, and all those lobbyists and their clients provide the fun. It won't change anytime soon.

However, he notes an important and counterintuitive change that President Trump has made already: He lifted Obama's restrictions on lobbyists serving in the administration, to the horror of the press, but at the same time, Trump banned people who *leave* his administration from engaging in lobbying for at least five years. Obama, in limiting lobbyists' ability to *enter* his administration, had it backward, says Abramoff.

You want people with knowledge of and experience in industry, for instance, to serve in government. What you do not want is them leaving and profiting in industry from their ties to (and residual influence over) government. Trump understands that the real source of corruption in the "revolving door" between government and business is people "cashing in" by exiting government. That's when they set up lucrative consultancies and work their old connections on the Hill to steer policy-making, including regulations and subsidies, in directions favorable to their new, postgovernment, private-sector clients.

Again, nothing wrong with business—but government is not creating a level playing field. Government as we now know it is the main thing tilting the playing field away from the average citizen. That's one of the reasons more and more average citizens see politics as rigged against them and hope Trump can do something to right the balance. They aren't viewing the conflict as capitalism versus socialism or right versus left so much as crony insiders (from government and business) versus everybody else. That's probably a more realistic description of the Swamp than you'd find in the usual political manifestos of activists from either party.

"Money buys access and influence," says Craig Holman of the liberal government-reform group Public Citizen. From his perspective, it's almost inevitable, and he may be right. The group he works for was started by Ralph Nader, a leftist and environmentalist I don't normally agree with. Yet in their recognition of how much corruption there is in the current political process, Nader and reformist liberals like Holman are on the right track.

Society won't function for long if we try to punish people for having money, as some on the left might like to do—but we can limit the temptation to use that money to influence government, in part by *limiting* the scope and power of government, as the Constitution originally intended. Then there's less reason to bribe and cajole politicians. Unfortunately, in recent decades, government has grown and grown, generating ever more places where it intersects with private activity and creates the temptation for bribery and collusion.

But to listen to the rhetoric of typical political campaigns, of course you'd think the only corruption is in the *other* party from whichever side you happen to be on. A politician willing to condemn the entire back-scratching culture of Washington is rare. While they're on the campaign trail, they usually only want you to notice the other side's scandals.

Red is associated with Republicans, and blue is associated with Democrats. Greed is pure green and pledges allegiance to no party. The power of greed can and does overwhelm players on both sides of the aisle, and the American people are undermined if they are represented by officials who weaken and succumb to greed's magnetic pull. Hard-earned tax dollars are sent by Americans to Washington, but greed gets its dirty little hands on those dollars over and over again until each dollar is worth only pennies—at the end of greed's wash and rinse cycles.

6. CAMPAIGN OF ERROR

One of the most detestable of mankind.
—MARTHA WASHINGTON ON THOMAS JEFFERSON

Most of the time, the public pays very little attention to the details of government. Campaign time is when the public wakes up and at least notices what politicians are saying, if not necessarily what they're actually doing. Campaign season is also when the contrast between politicians' loftiest claims and the most sordid accusations against them—often true—is most clearly on display. If the Swamp creatures are going to try rising above the Swamp or get sucked deeper into the morass, the campaign season is the best time to watch it happen.

"We have much work to do, because the truth is, we still live in a country where there are two different Americas," proclaimed Democratic vice presidential candidate Senator John Edwards at the Democratic convention in 2004, "one, for all of those people who have lived the American dream and don't have to worry, and another for most Americans, everybody else who struggle [*sic*] to make ends meet every single day. It doesn't have to be that way."

John Edwards later campaigned for the 2008 Democratic presidential primary on that theme of "two Americas," but he never seemed to understand the extent to which the two Americas are the corrupt world of politics on one hand and the real world of ordinary citizens on the other. He also, perhaps inevitably, turned out to be another phony moralist, one who was concealing a longtime mistress and a love child from his ailing wife.

From the public's perspective, the unraveling of Edwards began with a tabloid report in which an anonymous source alleged that Edwards had had an affair in 2007, in the early stages of his presidential campaign. Edwards denied it. The alleged mistress shortly thereafter announced she was pregnant—but not by Edwards, she at first claimed. Within a few months, the truth would come out. Within a few years, Edwards would be on trial for using hush money to cover up the scandal—and (although he denied it) being accused of hiring prostitutes around the same time, just in case there was anything left of his moral luster.

His mistress, Rielle Hunter, born Lisa Jo Druck, had been an actress and political video producer (and had glimpsed scandal before: Her father killed horses in an insurance-fraud scheme). She had also been the girlfriend of author Jay McInerney, inspiring a decadent and dangerous character named Alison Poole, who appeared as a cautionary figure in not one but two novels by his friend Bret Easton Ellis. That was a warning sign.

In 2006, she began creating viral YouTube videos for Edwards's emerging 2008 presidential campaign. In October 2007, she became the topic of a *National Enquirer* story alleging that she was pregnant with Edwards's child. The *Enquirer* is a tabloid, but it has a lower error rate than people give it credit for. Over the course of the next year, the truth came out in painful, slow servings—especially painful for Edwards's wife, Elizabeth, no doubt. Hunter claimed in December 2007 that she was indeed pregnant—but at first said the father was Edwards's staffer Andrew Young.

By the time of the 2008 primaries, the story was no longer just the stuff of tabloids, and the mainstream media were getting in on the speculation that Edwards was done for, with reports circulating that he had visited what was actually his child in Hunter's hotel. In August of that year, Edwards admitted having an affair with Hunter but still denied fathering her child. In January 2009, Edwards admitted in a press conference that the child was his—at a time when his wife was also reported to be suffering from potentially terminal breast cancer.

By mid-2009, Edwards, still insisting in folksy, man-of-the-people fashion that he was "a sinner but not a criminal," was being investigated for possible criminal misuse of campaign funds, spending about $1 million to house Hunter and care for their child instead of buying campaign supplies and hiring staffers. All in all, maybe we're better off the Edwards campaign didn't spend the money getting him elected.

In early 2010, Elizabeth held a press conference to announce that she and John were separating. At roughly the same time, Andrew Young released a book about the scandal in which he admitted that he had been pressured by John Edwards to pretend that the child was his own, to cover up payments to Hunter, and to conceal the fact that Edwards had promised to marry Hunter with great fanfare once his wife died from her aggressive cancer. Whichever America John Edwards is from, it's not too classy.

By December 2010, Elizabeth Edwards passed away and John Edwards invited Hunter to move into his house in Elizabeth's place. For a short time, it appeared that the improbable couple might last and raise their child together. Things started to look shakier in mid-2012, when Hunter released her own book about the scandal, *What Really Happened: John Edwards, Our Daughter, and Me*, announcing on the day of its release that she and Edwards were breaking up.

Theirs was apparently a tenacious romance, though, and she later claimed the two of them were still romantically involved until at least 2015.

Edwards's political career has not been as enduring. He was indicted in 2011 over the diversion of funds, but the jury was deadlocked on most of the charges and found him not guilty on one. The Justice Department dropped the other charges. So, from appearing to be the compassionate conscience of his party, Edwards went in a few years to a man just happy not to be fined or in jail.

He has returned to being a lawyer, a common profession among the Swamp creatures for centuries now, and perhaps one that makes them a bit more cocky about playing fast and loose with the rules.

Campaign rhetoric soars and political figures make themselves out to be redeemers and moral paragons—even when they are deeply morally flawed. Secretly aware of their own shortcomings, they nonetheless dare to sell us on the idea that our own lives can be whipped into shape by giving them more power and money.

If we listened to all the negative things politicians say about each other, of course, we would be left trusting none of them—which might be wise. Edwards's out-of-wedlock child, for example, doesn't seem so unusual when you look at the long list of politicians who have either been proven to have illicitly fathered kids or who have at least been accused of it by their opponents.

Republican James Blaine, a former U.S. senator from Maine, nearly defeated Democrat Grover Cleveland in the 1884 presidential race in part because Blaine's campaign uncovered the fact that Cleveland had been romantically involved with a woman named Maria Crofts Halpin a decade earlier—and had paid her child support for a child she gave the last name Cleveland, in spite of which Cleveland maintained the child was not his. His story wasn't morally spotless, though, since he contended that Maria was sleeping with multiple men, including Cleveland and his law partner Oscar Folsom (the child's oddly ambiguous full name was Oscar Folsom Cleveland). Cleveland contended that it seemed most appropriate for him to pay for the child's upkeep, since he was the only bachelor among her set of lovers and would—it was thought—create the least scandal. If only he had known.

As rumors about the child's paternity spread, Maria clumsily attempted to escape the scandal by releasing an affidavit claiming that there was no doubt Folsom was the father—and blaming Cleveland for suggesting otherwise. Blaine's supporters not only spread rumors that Cleveland had a bastard in Buffalo but that Maria had been pressured into fleeing to an asylum. Cleveland lamely responded that her whereabouts were no longer known, though he was quite bold in admitting the details of the situation, without delaying or attempting a cover-up the way Edwards did over a century later.

Blaine's supporters were delighted and soon created cartoons and posters for the campaign depicting Cleveland's forlorn son calling out, "Ma! Ma! Where's my pa?" That soon became a chant that haunted Cleveland at public gatherings. Nonetheless, he squeaked to victory, the only Democrat besides Woodrow Wilson to win the presidency between the start of the Civil War and the 1932 election of Franklin Roosevelt.

After winning the White House, Cleveland supporters would respond to the "Ma! Ma! Where's my pa?" taunt with the retort "Gone to the White House, ha ha ha!" Scandal had both hurt and helped Cleveland, though: "Mugwump" Republicans (their nickname a mangled version of a Native American word meaning "important person") had voted for Cleveland due to Blaine's own ethical problems, which were of greater significance for public policy purposes. He was accused of favoritism in the awarding of public railroad contracts.

Illicit children are a frequently recurring theme in election campaigns, and outing other candidates' estranged half-black children seems to be an especially popular tactic, premised on the idea that the other team—not one's own!—is a bunch of gullible racists, as sometimes of course they are. The biracial illegitimate child is a deeply cynical two-pronged tactic: Some voters may be appalled that an innocent child was abandoned. Others may be appalled that taboo color lines have been crossed.

Optimists might like to imagine that politicians and political appointees settle down to the serious business of governing once the heat of the campaign season is over, but that's not true. The bickering never stops, not even in the middle of a crisis such as a war, and it used to be much more common for members of the cabinet to argue with each other and with individual members of Congress publicly. Nowadays, there is at least an effort to keep up a "united front" that makes relatively graceful dismissal from a cabinet more likely than protracted infighting.

Lincoln's secretary of war, Simon Cameron, resigned in 1862 after corruption charges that inspired one congressmen, Radical Republican Thaddeus Stevens of Pennsylvania, to say—feigning an attempt to be positive about Cameron—"I don't think he would steal a red-hot stove." When criticized for the statement, the congressman responded by withdrawing it, without further clarification. Stevens told President Lincoln, "I believe I told you he would not steal a red-hot stove. I will now take that back."

Rumors of Cameron's corruption stretched back before he was awarding military contracts in sweetheart deals, to his days as a Democratic commissioner for Winnebago Indian affairs under President Van Buren in 1838, a position that afforded ample opportunity to misallocate Native American wealth. (Cameron's later switch from the Democrats to the Native American Party should not be seen as a change of heart: In those days, *Native American* meant anyone born here and was a rallying cry against immigrants. His newly adopted party became more commonly called the Know-Nothing Party.) Finally appointed by Lincoln to head the War Department at the most perilous time in the nation's history, Cameron soon doled out positions in his department to twenty Pennsylvania politicians and began awarding contracts and medals to friends and allies.

To delay accusations of corruption, Cameron cultivated the belief that he was merely forming a back-channels network of especially committed antislavery politicians who were trying to route around the relatively moderate Lincoln. Displeased and unconvinced of Cameron's higher motives, Lincoln transferred him to Russia for a brief, irrelevant stint as ambassador.

Cameron's own cynical quips about politics were hardly confidence boosters. He famously said, "An honest politician is one who, when he is bought, will stay bought." He may have been onto something. Economists have made serious arguments in more recent times that one reason political donations are not larger is simply that a politician, though bribable, is not a great investment. Even if you buy a reliably corrupt senator, the odds of him being able to enact the program you want him to, which may require the assent of several other legislators and even the president, are still fairly small. In other words, the bribe is far less bang for your buck than going through a lobbyist.

That's one more way in which the whole process gets skewed in favor of the big boys and the well connected: The rich have the money to gamble on trying to ply politicians, but you probably don't have that kind of cash to throw away, or connections to someone as cynical as Lincoln's secretary of war.

The public is in the dangerous habit of judging political figures mainly by their speeches and the sentiments expressed therein. But those speeches are often where the bulk of the lies happen, or at least the spin. Though Richard Nixon is sometimes remembered as being less media-savvy than John F. Kennedy, he well understood spin and the use of homespun imagery. When he was Eisenhower's vice presidential running mate and had to explain just how small and inconsequential some gifts he'd accepted from donors after an earlier Senate run really were—totaling some $18,000 and including what he described as a humble "Republican cloth" coat for his wife—he seized the opportunity to tell the world about his intention to keep one gift he'd received, while returning most of the money for the sake of appearances, if not out of any legal necessity. That one gift?

As he steadily intoned in a campaign-saving half-hour TV address from California:

> It was a little cocker spaniel dog in a crate . . . sent all the way from Texas. Black and white spotted. And our little girl—Tricia, the six-year-old—named it Checkers. And you know, the kids, like all kids, love the dog and I just want to say this right now, that regardless of what they say about it, we're going to keep it.

Sixty-five years later, the adorable dog is about the only thing anyone remembers from that speech, which is exactly how Nixon wanted it.

Nixon wasn't the biggest BS artist in government in Eisenhower's day. A contender for that prize has to be Representative Douglas Stringfellow of Utah, who served one term in the House but abandoned his 1954 reelection campaign when it was revealed he had exaggerated the heroism of his war record, a major no-no in the days of General Ike, especially from one of Ike's fellow Republicans.

Stringfellow didn't just paint overly colorful pictures of his battle prowess, though. He went further. He pretended to be paraplegic to garner sympathy votes. That takes a certain level of commitment, oddly enough, albeit commitment to a con.

Stringfellow was one of those baffling cases where it would seem there was no necessity to lie and yet he couldn't resist doing so. He really had been in the Army Air Forces, as it was then called, for three years of World War II. Furthermore, he was wounded from a mine explosion while in France. That's heroism enough for one lifetime, by most people's standards. But Stringfellow wanted more.

In Stringfellow's retelling, he had also been an agent of the OSS (the Office of Strategic Services, precursor to the Central Intelligence Agency) and had even been on a secret mission to rescue the German atomic scientist and anti-Nazi Otto Hahn behind enemy lines. Cool! But that's still not all. Instead of admitting that a mine caused his limp, he claimed he'd been horribly tortured after the Hahn mission, imprisoned in Bergen-Belsen Prison. Lying in his prison bed, racked with pain, he had undergone a religious experience, which gave him the strength to endure until anti-Nazi agents within Germany were able to smuggle him out of the prison, enabling him to live until being awarded a Silver Star for his service. His constituents loved it. Sounds like the Saturday-morning adventure movie serials of the day—unfortunately, that was not a coincidence.

Well, maybe some wartime tall tales weren't such a big problem. After all, so long as he stuck to the important issues of the day—like the Cold War and Jim Crow—he might have been able to casually disavow his military exaggerations at some point along the way. Alas, Stringfellow repeated and embellished the lies, getting the blessings of the Mormon Church (which was as duped as everyone else) to take his show on the road, preaching about the importance of his religious experience in prison to his survival.

The broader public wasn't spared Stringfellow's yarns either. He was on the popular television show *This Is Your Life*, commemorated as a war hero and showered with praise. Except this was not his life. This was not anyone's life. His Democratic opponents dug into his past and discovered his lies, and they didn't end with his wartime exploits. They also found out he'd never gone to Ohio State University as he'd claimed, nor the University of Cincinnati. Soon, the Mormon Church pressured him to make a public confession, and the Republican Party replaced him on the November 1954 ballot, just sixteen days before the election.

He became a radio announcer under a pseudonym and a landscape painter but never again entered electoral politics. He was only forty-four when he died of a heart attack, twelve years after the scandal.

Keep some of the sordid tactics, heated rhetoric, and brazen lies of past campaigns in mind if you hear people panicking over the use of colorful phrases in our own day, like Trump's deployment of "nasty woman" against Hillary Clinton or "bad hombres" against, well, the truly bad hombres of violent Mexican drug cartels. Incivility existed in the Swamp long before Trump added a few choice wisecracks. Sometimes a harsh word is called for, after all. Can you really blame Trump, for instance, for tweeting "Why would anybody listen to Mitt Romney? He lost an election that should have easily been won against Obama. By the way, so did John McCain!"

It was Mark Twain who said, "Suppose you were an idiot, and suppose you were a member of Congress. But I repeat myself."

It was widely respected Senator Bob Dole of Kansas who, gazing upon former presidents Carter, Ford, and Nixon, reportedly muttered, "There they are: see no evil, hear no evil, and evil."

But then, even more well-liked Representative Jack Kemp of New York, who would become Dole's 1996 running mate, said of

Dole, "In a recent fire, Bob Dole's library burned down. Both books were lost. And he hadn't even finished coloring one of them."

Pretty harsh—but then, consider some of the harsh things said by our esteemed Founding Fathers and their associates.

John Adams called Hamilton "the bastard brat of a Scotch peddler"—which was technically accurate but not meant to sound very nice. He repeated the colorful phrase in multiple letters, including one to Thomas Jefferson.

Jefferson in turn had some supporters who weren't so crazy about Adams, one screed calling him a "hideous hermaphroditical character, which has neither the force and firmness of a man, nor the gentleness and sensibility of a woman."

Adams's campaign responded that Jefferson was a "mean-spirited, low-lived fellow, the son of a half-breed Indian squaw, sired by a Virginia mulatto father." An early glimpse of those race-mixing accusations that keep cropping up in campaigns! I hope those anti-race-mixing insults never reached the ears of Sally Hemings, since she bore Jefferson several mixed-race children, and it's slavery, not unusual genetics, that should have been seen as offensive here.

Campaigners for Adams's son John Quincy Adams carried on the family tradition of colorful insults, declaring Andrew Jackson and his wife "adulterers" and her a prostitute because of the debate over the timing of her earlier divorce. You may recall that Jackson thought stress over those accusations contributed to the early death of his wife, Rachel.

With their tendency toward viciousness and unnecessary fighting, it's amazing, really, that the creatures of the Swamp ever manage to band together and work as a team. But they do—otherwise they would never be able to form corrupt political machines. And that's when the real dirty work starts.

7. MACHINES IN THE SWAMP

The political machine triumphs because it is a united minority acting against a divided majority.

—WILL DURANT

The bigger the machine, the more grease it requires to keep the thing moving.

If individual politicians at times behave like criminals, and you therefore expect groups of politicians to act like organized crime, you'd be correct. Unfortunately (for American taxpayers), there are too many examples of "political crime machines" to include them all, but some are so egregious they cannot be ignored.

We can't peer inside the Clintons' heads and know whether they are motivated by lust for power, material greed, and reckless lust— or a burning desire to improve the lot of humanity. We can't know whether their Clinton Foundation functions as a giant, global bribe-taking machine—but we can see what happens to the stream of massive donations to the Clinton Foundation at times when the Clintons' political power appears to be waning. (It shrinks.)

The Clinton Foundation took in about $300 million per year while Hillary Clinton was secretary of state (ending in 2013), often from nations with which the State Department had dealings, including millions from sometimes-hostile nations in the Arab world, but the *New York Post* reported that in 2015, after she had left the State Department, "Contributions fell by 37% to $108 million, down from $172 million in 2014, according to the group's latest tax filings." The Clintons' revenue from speeches—another convenient and legal way for rich hosts to curry favor with politicians—fell from $3.6 million in 2014 to $357,000 in 2015.

Would Clinton Foundation donations and the Clintons' speaking fees have shot back up if Hillary were elected president? We don't know. One arm of the foundation, the Clinton Global Initiative, began shutting down two months after the election. Peter Schweizer's book *Clinton Cash* chronicles, though, how money to the Clintons was sometimes timed very closely to shifts in State Department policy, such as the approval of uranium sales to Russia immediately after a $500,000 payment by a Kremlin-linked bank to Bill Clinton for a speech and millions in donations from the Russian company Uranium One to the Clinton Foundation.

Hillary's campaign chair, John Podesta, also had odd Russia ties, specifically millions of dollars' worth of shares in the Putin-linked Joule Unlimited, which he did not fully disclose during the presidential campaign, eventually transferring his shares to his daughter.

From the very start of the Clintons' time in government, the two seem to have recognized the profit opportunities afforded by the overlap between the public and private sectors. During Bill's stint as Arkansas attorney general from 1977 to 1979, Hillary enjoyed what she still claims was an astonishing run of good luck investing in cattle futures. There is a long history of metaphorical and sometimes literal "cattle trading" in politics, whereby politicians will offer each other goods such as cattle at a drastically discounted price as a reward for political support—but what Hillary did was the modern, Wall Street–style equivalent.

A lawyer for the most influential business in Arkansas, Tyson Foods, ostensibly acted as Hillary's guide as she gingerly poked her toe into the world of investing for the first time—and got such astonishingly good advice that the $1,000 she'd given the Tyson lawyer to oversee ballooned roughly a hundred times in value, leaving her with $98,540 in profit. Well done, Hillary! Except, obviously, what was going on here was merely a thinly veiled bribe, too big for any standard gift or donation rules but aimed at the relevant official's spouse instead of the attorney general himself—and disguised as something she had "earned." She later called it "beginner's luck."

Take it from me, as a commodity trader for the better part of two decades, this was no "beginner's luck"! I've traded all the commodities—cattle futures, oil, gold, corn, all of them—and winning or losing has nothing to do with luck. Winning in commodities takes a ton of work. You must study trends in pricing, trends in the labor markets, trends in the money markets. You *must* have a grasp of weather—yes, weather! Weather is a major factor in commodity prices. The more volatile the weather, the higher a commodity price will typically trend, because weather can damage crops (feed costs go up) and can kill livestock. Weather can wipe out oil installations, and energy is a level-one input to pricing almost every commodity on earth. The energy cost of bringing a product to market is integral to the price of the commodity.

The point I am trying to make is that there is *no way* Hillary Clinton got "lucky" with a string of commodity trading wins. The more likely scenario is that Mrs. Clinton's Tyson Foods "advisor" saw an opening to gain access to her husband, by then the governor, who likely could be very helpful to Tyson Foods with land grants and some regulatory "looking away."

Then the "advisor" likely ate the losses and dropped the wins into Hillary's account.

On some level, Hillary probably thinks she did earn it. Politics takes effort, after all, even if it's a game played with other people's money and doesn't pay off for the commoners quite the way it does for the political royalty. She and Bill may even worry they still haven't gotten their fair share. The Clintons nearly got their hands on the most lucrative political prize of all, the White House, for a second time in the 2016 election. Having failed to do so, they may find their "nonprofit" activities a bit less remunerative in the future.

The Clintons were, for a time, the avant-garde of "machine" politics. Instead of the smoke-filled rooms and ward bosses of old, they had charmed an array of public relations firms, media figures, international nonprofits, corporate boards, and politicians of nearly all nations, democratic and decidedly undemocratic. Hillary's birthplace, Chicago, is known for politics that is a bit closer to old-fashioned, bare-knuckle, friend-or-foe machines than to the avant-garde. Back in 1996, Chicago-area rising star (and Hillary's future boss) Barack Obama won his first election, to the Illinois state senate, by getting his serious opponent disqualified on technicalities.

Obama and other lawyers on his team managed to find enough irregularities or debatable signatures on the nomination petitions of all three of his Democratic primary opponents—including that of the incumbent, Alice Palmer, seemingly a longtime Obama ally in Chicago leftist activism—to get them tossed off the ballot. After he won the Democratic nomination with ease, and his district was overwhelmingly Democratic, the general election was then a breeze. His rise had more to do with lawyering than being raised up by the democratic masses.

So often in politics, the speeches are pretty but serve mainly as a distraction from the favor-granting and deal-making that really make the Swamp percolate.

In the early days of the republic, one of the greatest sources of temptation for corrupt politicians was the ambiguity about how to carve up the vast lands opening in the West.

Future president Zachary Taylor, who had first made a name for himself in the War of 1812 and also shone in the 1830s in the Black Hawk War and Second Seminole War, was himself instrumental in expanding the United States' hold on the Southwest, defeating Mexico's Santa Ana in battle in 1847 during the Mexican-American War. Those deeds helped spur clubs promoting his candidacy for president in 1848, even though (like many military men) he had avoided expressing any partisan political beliefs prior to being drawn into electoral politics. He called himself a Jeffersonian democrat aligned with the United States' short-lived Whig Party (which would dissolve and be partly succeeded by the Republican Party a few years after Taylor's brief presidency ended in 1850). With admirable humility, Taylor believed in a cautious president and a strong cabinet.

Unfortunately, some of his cabinet members saw opportunity in their elevated status—and opportunity in those ambiguously carved-up lands out west and to the south. In the territory that would become Georgia, Irish immigrant George Galphin, who died in 1780, had owned a very large tract of land, one the U.S. government seized after the Revolutionary War. For seventy years, Galphin's family had fought the U.S. government in court for compensation. Finally, the governor of Georgia, George Crawford, entered the dispute on the side of the family, securing about $200,000 from the federal government for them—and keeping about half for himself in the name of the Georgia territory.

This fiscal sleight of hand in 1850 might never have attracted much attention had not Crawford become President Taylor's secretary of war the previous year. Crawford's elevated status then combined with the decades-long public interest in the almost-legendary Galphin estate dispute to produce a great public outcry. Crawford resigned but managed to elude a public investigation or punishment in part because the Taylor presidency soon came to an end. In July 1850, after only sixteen months in office, Zachary Taylor died of an undetermined intestinal ailment.

Crawford, though hounded into resignation, lived off his half of the Galphin money for the rest of his life.

Feuding cabinet members were a normal part of politics back then, a drastic contrast with today's usually in-sync cabinets. One popular way to try avoiding conflict, of course, is to appoint your friends and close allies. And in the nineteenth century, as well as today, presidents knew they could technically get around the need for Senate approval by making recess appointments when Congress wasn't around to complain.

President Andrew Johnson, who had been Abraham Lincoln's vice president, used his recess-appointment powers to replace his secretary of war, Edwin Stanton, whom Johnson regarded as one of several military men too bent on punishing the South in the wake of the Civil War. Johnson was already on thin ice with the Republican-dominated, antislavery postwar Congress—and impeachment charges were considered against him in committee even before his actual impeachment—due to him allowing former Confederate president Jefferson Davis to go free on bail. (The investigating committee found that Johnson had favored prosecuting Davis, though, and so did not press for Johnson's removal.)

With Stanton ousted, Ulysses S. Grant reluctantly agreed to serve as Johnson's new secretary of war until Congress returned from its

summer recess, and he followed Johnson's orders to pardon Confederate soldiers and remove several harsh military governors over-
seeing the Reconstruction of the South.

Congress did not return to session in a forgiving mood, and on
December 7, 1867, the Judiciary Committee voted to recommend
impeaching Johnson—which, as with Bill Clinton over a century
later, means merely that charges potentially resulting in his removal
would be weighed in Congress, not that he necessarily would
ultimately be removed from office—but the congressional vote for
impeachment at that time failed, by a vote of 57–108. Nonetheless,
the Senate reinstated Stanton as secretary of war the following year.
Johnson did not relent and ordered Stanton removed again in favor
of army general Lorenzo Thomas.

This is where the scandal became truly messy.

Stanton refused to leave office, and on February 24, 1868, after
flirting with the possibility twice before, the House voted to im-
peach Johnson, making him the first president (and to date one of
only two presidents) to be impeached, specifically for violation
of the Tenure of Office Act, which prevents the president from firing certain officeholders without Senate approval. To the great annoyance of Johnson and great fascination of the public, the resulting
trial stretched on for three months. Johnson's lawyers—who argued
that the act did not fully apply, since Stanton had been appointed
by the deceased Lincoln, not by Johnson himself—told Johnson
not to talk in public about the case and urged him not to appear in
Congress while it debated the issue. Johnson took their advice, a
degree of restraint difficult to imagine in our own day.

In the end, the trial process became a scandal unto itself, with
the verdict partly determined by wheeling and dealing among
members of Congress, who were wary of making the president pro
tempore of the Senate (then next in the line of presidential succes-
sion), Benjamin Franklin Wade, the president. Wade was a Radical

Republican who was not only in favor of taking a tough line with the South but also against such innovations as women's suffrage. He was as unsettling to Congress in his own way as the perceived coddling of the South by Johnson.

The House abandoned its prosecution of Johnson after repeatedly falling one vote short of conviction. Stanton stepped down on May 26. And accusations that bribery had determined the impeachment outcome haunted Johnson for the remainder of his presidency. In November, he did not run for a second full term.

Ulysses S. Grant, who had been such a pillar of honorable commitment to duty while he was a political ping-pong ball under Johnson, saw several scandals during his own presidency after succeeding Johnson in 1869, including a district court judge impeached for drunkenness, members of Congress implicated in the Crédit Mobilier bribery scandal, and multiple cabinet members involved in bribery and kickback scandals, including the secretaries of the interior, navy, treasury, and war. Fittingly for the alcoholic Grant, whiskey taxes were at the center of a corruption ring that saw 110 people from or affiliated with the administration convicted.

In spite of all this, it is widely agreed that Grant, though he was an alcoholic, was not himself corrupt and approached the duties of his office with the methodical determination of an accomplished military man.

Some parts of the federal government may be more prone to inspire officials to corrupt behavior than others—to lend themselves naturally to being captured by political machines, as it were. It is not surprising, for instance, that the commissioner of Indian Affairs was forced to resign for corruption in 1880, one small footnote in a centuries-long story of U.S. government misbehavior regarding Native Americans.

Under Presidents Garfield and Arthur began a long tradition of postal service corruption and mismanagement—in a part of government that seems especially ripe for privatization in our own day! President Arthur's appointee for governorship of the Dakota Territory, Nehemiah Ordway, was also indicted and then removed from office by Arthur. He had racked up multiple accusations of misappropriation of funds and corruption, but what really turned political leaders in what is now South Dakota against him was his single-handed effort to move the territorial capital from Yankton to Bismarck. Such passions did the tug-of-war over the territorial capital ignite, it might be considered the nineteenth-century Dakotas version of Jerusalem, which most of the world tiptoes around mentioning as the capital of Israel, lest the Palestinians, who still claim land there, be offended.

As the twentieth century dawned, some political figures finally began figuring out how to use widespread political corruption itself as a source of power.

A federal district attorney appointed by President McKinley, John Hicklin Hall of Oregon, for instance, used blackmail against his opponents, gleaning from his legal work secrets usable for his illegal pressure campaigns. Once more, land was the great prize sought by the corrupt, and when several local officials in Oregon gained fraudulent possession of a vast tract of Oregonian land for a private front company, Hall foot-dragged in prosecuting them and instead selectively threatened to divulge damaging information about people involved in the land deal unless they aided him in his own political projects. Teddy Roosevelt, having become president upon McKinley's assassination by an anarchist, removed Hall from office.

Thanks to such stories—spread by the increasingly efficient yellow journalism of the day—there was a rising cynicism about politics, a counterpoint to the cynicism among the general public about big business in the Gilded Age.

The perception of widespread political corruption—and the sheer pettiness of gangster-like political "machines" such as Tammany Hall in New York—contributed in the late nineteenth and early twentieth century to the rise of the Progressive Era. One of the early Progressives' animating ideas was the conviction that less reliance on elected officials and more reliance on the scientific and technocratic expertise of appointed bureaucrats would make the world more fair and rational. This was seen as a moderate, mainstream alternative to the socialism sweeping Europe.

Unfortunately, even this milder version of big government led to great waste and inefficiency—and of course vast new opportunities for cronyism, favoritism, and misallocation of resources, albeit disguised with more humanitarian and "scientific"-sounding rhetoric. As James A. Morone 1990 book *The Democratic Wish* argues, time and again in American history, the longing for political reform simply led to even bigger, more distant government and new layers of bureaucracy.

With new layers—and whole new kinds—of modern bureaucracy, of course, would come new opportunities for corruption and new resulting scandals. Despite the naive hopes of the Progressives, the twentieth century would not see the Swamp cleansed of corruption and irrationality. Instead, the Swamp and its increasingly smooth-talking, media-savvy, number-crunching inhabitants would *evolve*.

8. BIG GOVERNMENT, BIG SCANDALS

You know I am a juggler, and I never let my right hand know what my left hand does. I'm perfectly willing to mislead and tell untruths.
—FRANKLIN D. ROOSEVELT

Teddy Roosevelt, the first U.S. president to enter the White House in the twentieth century, was not a cautious man. As he put it, "In any moment of decision, the best thing you can do is the right thing, the next best thing is the wrong thing, and the worst thing you can do is nothing."

He was an athlete, scientist, historian, big game hunter, doting father, soldier, and would-be Progressive reformer wielding the "bully pulpit" of the presidency (not to mention a famous "big stick") as if he could almost single-handedly whip foreign armies, domestic corporations resistant to regulation, and government corruption into shape.

Even in defeat, as in 1913 after he lost his third bid for the White House, Roosevelt was not a man to fade idly into retirement. He took a trip to Brazil and accepted the Brazilian government's offer to change his original plans and, instead of making a speaking tour, to accompany explorers of a newly discovered river, then called ominously the River of Doubt and since renamed Rio Roosevelt, taking with him his son. Of the nineteen men in the exploration party, three died along the way, one being abandoned by the party for murdering another.

The entire group nearly perished from hunger and malaria along the route, and Roosevelt's own health never fully recovered—but that did not stop him from speaking to scientific societies in his remaining five years of life about the river expedition, fueled partly by anger that some people doubted his discoveries. Teddy was a combative man in a tough era, one when it still seemed that sufficient determination and common sense were bound to lead to ennobling outcomes.

It was an era for bold action, leaps into the future—some good, some catastrophic—in areas ranging from politics to imperial warmaking to art and architecture. The first decade of the twentieth century saw the rise of automobile assembly lines, zeppelins, airplanes, and Einstein's theory of relativity. The Panama Canal was planned. The tangled alliances that would lead to World War I were put in place as well.

It seemed as if anything might be possible in the new century—and to the Progressive reformers' minds, that included driving corruption out of politics. To them, it was another lingering defect of the past to be ironed out by a new wave of technocratic efficiency.

But the Swamp can't be paved over that easily. The founding Progressive presidents of both parties, Republican Teddy Roosevelt and Democrat Woodrow Wilson, still had scandals during their administrations, pretenses of rationality notwithstanding.

One reason for enduring—even increasing—scandal over the course of the twentieth century was that the sheer size of government, going from about 8 percent of GDP at the start of the century to about 40 percent by the end, meant that it became more important than ever before to wield influence over government. It could tax, regulate, or subsidize more aspects of your life than ever before. By contrast, one of the biggest scandals in the presidency of late-nineteenth-century president Benjamin Harrison had been that federal spending, fueled partly by comfortable budget surpluses, exceeded $1 billion for the first time.

Those days would soon seem quaint.

As Roosevelt said, observing the rising power of the bureaucratic elite, "A man who has never gone to school may steal from a freight car, but if he has a university education, he may steal the whole railroad."

Part of the Progressive Era dream was to make big government a partner with big business. How could that possibly go wrong?

Well, it could go wrong like the career of Representative H. Burd Cassel of Pennsylvania. He was a Republican member of Congress and sometime ally of Teddy Roosevelt but also the president of the Pennsylvania Construction Company—and one of several people who were convicted of paying bribes to secure some $2 million in funding for the creation of gleaming, modern electrical fixtures for the refurbished Pennsylvania state capitol, as revealed in what *The New York Times* described in 1907 as "testimony of a sensational character" before an investigating committee.

The so-called Oregon land scandal, in which the old practice of bribing public officials to get grants to western land continued into the twentieth century, came to a head on Teddy Roosevelt's watch, but a U.S. district attorney who was convicted in the affair, John Hicklin Hall, had been appointed by McKinley. The scheme didn't originate with him. In fact, he was supposed to be prosecuting the people involved. Instead, he blackmailed them, threatening to prosecute if they didn't pay up.

The same scandal took down Senator John Hipple Mitchell of

Oregon—or would have had he not died in 1905, after he was con-victed but before he could be sentenced, while he was appealing the conviction. That was Mitchell's final brush with scandal, though it was definitely not his first: Early in his Senate career in the 1870s, his enemies tried without success to drive him from the Senate by reminding the public he was a bigamist, had lived under an assumed name for a while, and had deserted from the army. None of it stopped him, just as it hadn't stopped him from becoming the pres-ident of the Oregon state senate.

Prior to all that, he'd been ousted from his job as a schoolteacher for having an affair with a fifteen-year-old student. At least he went on to marry her—and another woman to boot. They named a town after him in 1873, too. Mitchell, Oregon, still exists, population 130.

That means he fared better than another Roosevelt-era senator, Joseph R. Burton of Kansas, who, during his first term—which be-gan in 1901—accepted a $2,500 bribe from a company running a get-rich-quick scam to defend it from the U.S. Post Office, which wanted to revoke its right to use the mail. In 1904, he was fined $2,500 and sentenced—after a venue-based appeal and retrial in D.C. that reached the same verdict—to six months in jail. His sec-ond appeal, to the Supreme Court, was in vain. In mid-1906, he resigned from the Senate in disgrace—and returned to practicing law.

As Roosevelt put it, "When they call the roll call in the Senate, they do not know whether to call 'present' or 'not guilty.'"

Roosevelt himself, though he may have had more respect for U.S. laws than some of his associates, was arguably a source of greater moral transgressions. Roosevelt was an unapologetic imperialist, a forerunner, really, of the border-disregarding globalists of our own century. He knew that a Panama Canal could greatly simplify the flow of trade from the Pacific, but one small problem stood in the way of the project: not the vast expense or the horrible working conditions that would go on to kill twenty-two thousand people in the process of completing the canal but rather the government of Colombia, which at that time included the land that is now Panama.

Since the Colombian government wasn't cooperating, it would just have to be overthrown and Panama allowed to secede with the aid of the U.S. Army. As a breakaway revolutionary junta took control of Panama City in late 1903, the USS *Nashville* was sent to prevent Colombian troops disembarking in Colón to suppress the secession. Roosevelt claimed the United States was merely functioning like a neutral referee, safeguarding the multinational railway left behind by the French but still in use for the construction of the canal.

American military aid to the Panamanian secessionists was neither the first nor the last time the United States would intervene in Latin American politics with a disingenuous public rationale, and it didn't only create debate in the United States and Latin America; it contributed to over a century of resentment in Latin America against its pushy northern neighbor. But TR got what he wanted. Panama became an independent nation, and—more important for U.S. purposes—TR got his canal.

For decades prior to President Trump taking office, Americans tended to assume right-wingers were often restrictive of sexual activity such as homosexuality and in favor of military interventionism. We also tended to assume left-wingers would favor increased sexual freedom but vastly expanded government spending as well.

Unfortunately, during the twentieth century, we usually ended up with the worst elements of both right and left prevailing: more spending, more war, and despite an increasingly tolerant popular culture, occasional crusades against sex, drugs, or other personal liberties. You couldn't ask for a better example of all those forces coming together than the investigations during Woodrow Wilson's presidency of homosexuality in the navy.

The investigators were appointed by big-government booster extraordinaire (and future president) Franklin Delano Roosevelt, then secretary of the navy.

It all began in Newport, Rhode Island, not usually thought of as a den of iniquity, where in 1919 navy chief machinist's mate Ervin Arnold discovered the local army/navy YMCA and the Newport Art Association were immersed in a gay subculture (those Village People songs sixty years later weren't completely fictional). Alarmed by this breach of military protocols, Arnold paid visits to the establishments and reported back to the navy about sex parties, homosexuality, transvestism, and frequent drug and alcohol use going on there.

A court of inquiry was assembled, which concluded still more investigation was warranted, and got the approval of FDR, who asked Attorney General A. Mitchell Palmer to look into the clubs. Palmer, interestingly, didn't think the matter worthy of resources and so kicked the investigation back down to machinist's mate Ervin Arnold himself, who, as it happened, had previously been a Connecticut state detective—perhaps a bit more prone to peek into things than was truly necessary.

Arnold proceeded to hire about a dozen young, good-looking men to infiltrate the clubs and directly participate in the illegal activities. They reported back to Arnold in detail about their sexual encounters with other men at the club. As a result, some fifteen sailors were arrested. A three-week trial ensued, during which Arnold's investigators appeared as witnesses and described their own homosexual conduct in great detail—as evidence against the accused men. Seventeen sailors were court-martialed for "scandalous conduct," including sodomy, and most were sentenced to a naval prison as a result, in some cases after having already spent months imprisoned without charges (two were discharged and two more found innocent), though the judge, seemingly sympathetic to the accused men, had urged the jury to take the witness/investigators' duplicitous behavior into account.

The investigation was condemned by the *Providence Journal* and by local Episcopal clergy, who wrote a letter to President Wilson calling the investigators' methods "deleterious and vicious." FDR was listening. He was angered by the investigation's reckless tactics and worried that they might even discourage future navy recruitment. Even a century ago, government misbehavior was coming to be seen as a bigger scandal than illicit sex, which is probably for the best.

Roosevelt soon escaped the scandal by leaving his position as secretary of the navy to become the Democratic vice presidential nominee in 1920, running alongside presidential candidate James Cox. They lost in a landslide, and to add to FDR's pain, he was condemned by the Senate Committee on Naval Affairs the following year, in a report saying the homosexuality investigation "violated the code of the American citizen and ignored the rights of every American boy who enlisted in the navy to fight for his country" and called FDR's own conduct "reprehensible."

FDR was in no moral position to criticize others' sexual conduct, either: Eleanor had discovered one of his extramarital affairs in 1916, during World War I, which may have distracted him at least a little from more important global affairs. Somehow, he remains a great liberal hero to this day.

The Progressive Era didn't stop the usual parade of bribery and favor-granting that makes up most of the business in the Swamp.

During Taft's presidency, just prior to Wilson's 1912 election, Senator William Lorimer of Illinois, nicknamed "the Blond Boss" in Chicago, was expelled from the Senate for accepting bribes and buying votes—and his own election was declared invalid as a result. Leaving the Senate in disgrace, he went into banking.

Meanwhile, an Arizona senator, Ralph Cameron, attempted to buy up mining rights in lands surrounding the Grand Canyon in a bid to eventually control access to the canyon itself, a pretty shocking idea at a time when TR was so brazenly turning vast swaths of western land into national parks and spurring the emergence of modern conservationism—unless of course one takes the cynical view that both the Camerons and TRs of this world are all really engaged in self-serving land grabs, which might resolve the apparent contradiction.

But there is a bit more to Cameron than just a latecomer political opportunist. As historian Douglas Strong recounts, Cameron worked for thirty years before the scandal to develop and control the South Rim of the Grand Canyon. He'd been fascinated by the place since prospectors first ventured down into it in the 1880s and stagecoaches of tourists came to gaze upon it in awe. He fought off companies like the Santa Fe Railroad to fulfill his own vision of a hotel there—and fended off federal government influence as well. When it looked like that might not work, he began strategically locating mines in the canyon so he could claim the land around them. He was a self-serving, scandalous figure, yet you almost have to admire his drive and gumption.

Similarly, scandal is not the only metric by which to judge a politician or a presidency, of course.

It could be argued that no president was more conducive to peace and prosperity than Wilson's Republican successor, Warren G. Harding, who had beaten the Cox-FDR ticket in 1920, but is now rather unfairly remembered most for the bribe-taking, corrupt administration officials who surrounded him in D.C.—from the Teapot Dome gang who leased oil fields to private companies without competitive bidding in exchange for bribes (leading to the conviction of Interior Secretary Albert Bacon Fall) to the Office of

Alien Property official convicted of trying to sell as his own some patents that had been seized from Germans during World War I.

Harding was the first president to have a director of the Bureau of Veterans Affairs, and the bureau was no more pristine then than it is today: That first director ended up doing a two-year stint in prison for bribery.

Andrew Mellon was the treasury secretary during and long after Harding's presidency, and he embodied the perverse incentives at work during Prohibition, securing a medical permit for the alcohol company he had co-owned to continue operating, even as smaller producers were fined and jailed across the country. One member of Congress was convicted of violating alcohol Prohibition and resigned in 1926, too, by which time Harding had died, having served only two years as president, and had been succeeded by quiet conservative Calvin Coolidge.

The nature of D.C.'s scandals changes with the nation's changing mores and laws. Coolidge, in his notoriously low-key way, was something of a last gasp of the nation's old Christian politeness and laissez-faire economic views. "The chief business of the American people is business," as he put it. But both morals and business were coming to be seen more and more as political rather than purely private activities, and that would change the nature of the political scandals that arose around them.

One member of Congress, Representative Thomas L. Blanton, was nearly expelled in 1921 for entering "obscene" material into the Congressional Record itself—namely, a letter (with redactions) recounting something a foulmouthed (by the standards of the day) union member had reportedly said to a government printer, which is: "G-d D--n your black heart, you ought to have it torn out of you, you u------ s-- of a b----. You and the Public Printer has no

sense. You k---- his a-- and he is a d----d fool for letting you do it."
The House voted 313–1 to expunge the letter from the Congressional Record, nearly voted to expel Blanton (falling eight votes short),
and voted unanimously to censure him. The republic endured.

More serious by the standards of our own day were the 1926
impeachment of a judge for accepting an interest-free loan and the
1929 censure of a senator, Hiram Bingham of Connecticut, for
putting a manufacturing organization lobbyist on his staff. These
cases are probably more representative of the culture of government/
business cronyism we've grown accustomed to over the past century.
That creates problems bigger than mild swearing.

The complexity of the big government that arose in the twentieth century not only created more opportunities for graft, it also
created new layers of bureaucracy unlike anything that had existed
in the eighteenth or nineteenth centuries. Bureaucracies are terrible
at inspiring individual initiative and accountability—which is why
individuals in the marketplace get more work done—but bureaucracies are fantastic for shifting blame and obscuring details. Thus
we are so often left asking, "Who knew what when?" in the wake
of modern government scandals.

Sometimes opaque bureaucracy combines with old-fashioned criminal mischief to leave us with scandals that are never resolved, ones
that become historical mysteries. Though it is not as often recalled
as FDR's Supreme Court–packing scheme (or even his struggles with
bad publicity over the Newport investigation), a constitutional crisis of a different kind was feared during his presidency when J.
Edgar Hoover, the long-serving FBI director, was suspected of having a hand in the 1936 death of a Democratic representative from
Washington State serving his second term, with whom Hoover had
been at odds and who plunged unexpectedly from a Seattle window to his death.

As the *Seattle Post-Intelligencer* recounted on August 8, 1936, "When Congressman Marion A. Zioncheck killed himself before her eyes last night, something snapped inside this young bride, the former Rubye Louise Nix. And in an instant, she was transformed from a brave, carefree, laughing girl into a grief-stricken woman, both as old and as ageless as death itself. All dressed in white for the postal employees banquet she had expected to attend with her husband, she presented the tragic picture of a bride at a funeral as restoratives were administered to her at King County Hospital, a few minutes after the suicide."

Most likely, Zioncheck himself had been in a manic state somewhere between despair and elation—probably convinced, as he had been for the preceding two years, both that he had a special calling to make society more fair and that nefarious forces (including Hoover's FBI) were arrayed against him. Perhaps as he edged closer to the window, he thought defiantly that even suicide should not be used to smear his reputation. He had suggested in a public speech called "Who's Crazy?" that society, not his own erratic behavior, was irrational. He had a vision of a society in which all production would be based around best use (as determined by rational politicians like himself) rather than profit. Perhaps that fleeting glimpse of what he deemed a better world passed through his mind one last time as he went out through the window—and perhaps he glimpsed his wife as well and felt at least a twinge of regret.

Investigators found a barely grammatical, rambling suicide note inside Zioncheck's Arctic Building office. There was a lingering suspicion, though, that it had been faked—and that he had been pushed. But by whom? There were rumors it was Hoover. More likely, Zioncheck's plunge was the finale of a tragic history of mental illness, which had included episodes of public lunacy, such as dancing in fountains and driving on the lawn of the White House. In 1936, he told friends that he was deeply depressed over the unpopularity of some New Deal programs and might not seek reelection. His wife left him temporarily, and he ran through the streets of D.C. looking for her, ending up arrested and placed in a (literal) D.C. insane asylum, at which point poor Rubye returned to him out of concern for his well-being.

Transferred in the summer of 1936 to another asylum, this time in Maryland, Zioncheck managed to escape and fled back to Washington State. In early August, he plunged to his death before his wife's eyes. Surely, the unsurprising end result of a pattern of increasing mania, unless you were one of the people who suspected his death was payback for speeches he'd given in the House denouncing the heavy-handed tactics of Hoover—or for the time he sent a truckload of manure to Hoover's house.

Deservedly or not, the bigger a government gets and the more it intrudes into our lives, the more paranoid the public will understandably become about what each fresh scandal means. How corrupt are our public officials? What exactly are they up to in Washington? What on earth are they doing with our money? Are they insane? Are they cold-blooded enough to kill?

Few aspects of the twentieth century's fast-expanding government inspired more fear than the post–World War II military-industrial complex about which President Eisenhower warned. It produced heroes, but as we'll see, it also confronted Americans with the disquieting possibility of a giant bureaucracy that was corrupt, insane, and willing to kill all at the same time.

9. WAR MACHINE, SCANDAL MACHINE

In the councils of government, we must guard against the acquisition of unwarranted influence, whether sought or unsought, by the military-industrial complex. The potential for the disastrous rise of misplaced power exists and will persist.

—PRESIDENT DWIGHT D. EISENHOWER

It doesn't get much lower than overcharging the Defense Department while, in theory, it's trying to keep troops alive and the rest of America safe. But by now, it's routine.

We're not shocked anymore when, just to take fresh examples from 2017, a Pennsylvania defense contractor, Ibis Tek, has to issue a statement explaining that it wasn't directly responsible for the United States being charged $70 for $20 Humvee window installations. That was the doing, they say, of the brothers who previously owned the company.

Neither are we much shocked when a defense contractor at Camp Pendleton in California steals a quarter million dollars' worth of medical equipment. As KGTV in San Diego reported, this year saw a man plead guilty to being part of "a theft ring that saw $250,000 worth of medical equipment stolen, including anesthesia machines,

autoclaves, ventilators, ultrasound machines, defibrillators, and la-
ryngoscopes among other items meant for injured U.S. Marines
overseas."

The Pentagon has a lot of money, and ripping it off has been a
hobby for corrupt defense contractors for a long time now. Back in
the 1980s, much of the public found itself rooting for Ronald
Reagan's defense buildup to fend off the Communists but also growing increasingly wary of the Pentagon paying $640 for a plastic
toilet seat or $2,000 for an ordinary metal nut. Christopher Cerf
and Henry Beard published a *Pentagon Catalog* of absurdly over-
priced items for which the taxpayers had actually footed the bill,
including an ordinary claw hammer for $435 and a $37 screw from
aerospace company McDonnell Douglas.

As described by columnist Jack Smith, "Other items offered in
the catalogue include a $285 screwdriver, a $7,622 coffee maker,
a $387 flat washer, a $469 wrench, a $214 flashlight, a $437 tape
measure, a $2,228 monkey wrench, a $748 pair of duckbill pliers,
a $74,165 aluminum ladder, a $659 ashtray, and a $240 million
airplane." In today's prices, of course, the airplane almost sounds
reasonable.

The military is vitally necessary to maintain a secure America,
but it is also large and bureaucratic, like other parts of government. It
can be efficient and yet be wasteful. It can lose billions of dollars.
Metaphorically speaking, our nation's greatest heroes sometimes
fight for their lives not too far removed from the Swamp. Ripping
off the military is a very old tradition, but the problem escalated
after the vast increase in the size of our standing military during
and after World War II—and politicians, naturally, were among the
first to get their greedy, swampy mitts into the cookie jar.

Wasteful military spending isn't all the fault of the military itself,
much as the left might like to pretend it's unique to that part of government, a product of combative arrogance. The Pentagon keeps

telling Congress about bases and weapons systems that the military doesn't judge worth funding—but Congress keeps voting to fund them anyway. Why? Mainly because defense spending, while meant to protect the whole nation, gets spent in specific locations—specific congressional districts, that is. That means a program that's wasteful from the perspective of the U.S. population as a whole may be a sweet deal for the workers in one munitions factory or in a naval base that unexpectedly remains open.

And happy factory workers, base personnel, and surrounding local businesses translate into reelection votes for the Congress members who kept the programs alive, even if the resulting planes or ground vehicles aren't needed or could have been produced elsewhere at a quarter the cost. It's a disservice to our military to foist upon them any programs or equipment that exist mainly as congressional pork instead of as the wisest possible allocation of precious military resources. Rationally allocated, military spending is the very definition of a contribution to the "general welfare" as the Founding Fathers understood it—something that helps the nation as a whole, not just one tiny part of it—but turned into a parochial form of welfare, this noble function of government becomes one more form of cronyism.

When the Pentagon requested a process for closing unnecessary bases be implemented in 2015, members of the Senate Armed Services Committee from both parties were quick to tell the Pentagon it was wrong. "I come with a dislike for [that base-closing] process to begin with, so this is going to be a case of convincing me that it's the right thing to do," Senator Mike Rounds, Republican of South Dakota, told Pentagon officials, according to TheHill.com, while Senator Martin Heinrich, Democrat of New Mexico, said members of Congress are "skeptical about our bases being hollowed out."

Republican Kelly Ayotte, then a senator from New Hampshire, had the audacity to say the base-closing commission process was "created as a cop-out" to spare legislators from making the tough decisions about which bases to close, reported TheHill.com—yet she offered no evidence Congress *would* actually make those tough decisions if nonpartisan commissions didn't do it for them! Is the base-closing process supposed to save the Pentagon money or be a personal growth exercise for politicians?

More recently, the Office of the Special Inspector General for Afghanistan Reconstruction, commonly known as SIGAR, has kept tabs on wasteful programs and fraud, all at the expense of the U.S. taxpayer. In 2013, the Defense Department spent $486 million for twenty G222 aircraft for Afghanistan. The only problem is that these planes did not meet operational requirements in Afghanistan and were promptly discarded. After several years of sitting on the tarmac in Kabul, these planes were just turned into scrap metal! Almost half a billion dollars was spent on planes that were never used, then were abandoned and turned into scrap! John Sopko and Christopher Borgeson of SIGAR continue to regularly uncover countless examples of waste, fraud, and abuse!

One of the most notorious exploiters of the military money trough, Representative Andrew J. May of Kentucky, gained some notoriety as the possible cause of hundreds of U.S. war deaths even before he was charged with taking bribes.

A lawyer turned politician, May went on a Pacific war zone tour in 1943 and returned to give an ill-fated press conference in which he revealed the strategically significant fact that U.S. submarines were easily escaping Japanese depth charges due to the Japanese setting the fuses too short. Unaware just how deep U.S. subs could travel, the Japanese were detonating charges well above them. That changed not long after May's press conference, though it was never conclusively determined whether the Japanese made their adjustments based on May's overly revealing comments.

Whether or not May was responsible, ten U.S. submarines were sunk, killing some eight hundred men. But he wasn't done making his sad mark on military and political history.

Immediately after the war, a Senate investigating committee discovered that two New York businessmen, the Garsson brothers, who had been awarded big weapons-manufacturing contracts, had no prior weapons-manufacturing experience—yet they had gotten the contracts as a result of barrages of phone calls on their behalf to military officials by Representative May, then the chairman of the House Military Affairs Committee. An examination of the Garssons' finances revealed huge cash payments to May. He lost his 1946 re-election bid as a result. Nine months later, on July 3, 1947, May was convicted of accepting bribes, as were the Garsson brothers. May, who had so recently been influential in shaping the conduct of the biggest war the United States had ever fought, ended his congressional career in ignominy—but spent a mere nine months in prison. *Nine months!* May ripped off the men and women protecting his sorry butt—and furthermore may have caused hundreds of military casualties with a mortal case of loose lips.

This case of corruption may well be what occupied Eisenhower's mind a decade later when he warned of the growing influence of the military-industrial complex. Military spending isn't just big. Like everything else in Washington, it, too, is corrupt.

One reason corruption is so common in the Swamp is that we expect government to police itself.

That same 1946 election saw the Republicans take control of Congress, effectively ending the political era over which the late FDR held sway. Starting his sixth term was New Jersey congressman J. Parnell Thomas, and he was appointed chairman of the nine-year-old House Un-American Activities Committee, commonly known as HUAC. In this capacity, he rightly condemned the Communist threat (he wasn't just a dogmatic defense booster, either, and had urged General Eisenhower that same year to be quick in demobilizing the postwar military). Thomas railed against the New Deal as a legacy of FDR's purported Communist leanings, saying the New Deal had "sabotaged" capitalism. Thomas was also quite impatient with Hollywood witnesses' invocation of the Fifth Amendment right against self-incrimination in their testimony before the committee. That merciless streak would come back to haunt him. HUAC's activities are now sometimes remembered as a precursor to the often reckless and meandering investigatory zeal of anticommunist Senator Joseph McCarthy, though unlike Thomas, he was never officially associated with that committee.

Unfortunately for Thomas, his secretary, Helen Campbell, was engaged in an investigation of her own. Aware that newspaper columnists, no doubt eager to take the crusading anticommunist down a notch or two, had been writing about rumors of Thomas being corrupt, Campbell mailed syndicated columnist Drew Pearson accounting records from Thomas's congressional office, showing he had been receiving kickbacks from a woman ostensibly hired to be a clerk, Myra Midkiff, who'd had a do-nothing job with Thomas since 1940. Pearson wrote about the scam in 1948, and Thomas resigned from Congress in 1950, invoking his Fifth Amendment right against self-incrimination, to the amusement of his critics, in a grand jury investigation.

He went on to be tried and sentenced to a year and a half in jail, ending up in the same prison as two screenwriters, Ring Lardner Jr. and Lester Cole, who had been among the so-called Hollywood Ten jailed for their refusal to answer questions put to them by Thomas's committee. After prison, Thomas, long known to scan the newspapers for negative mentions of him or HUAC, gave up on politics and started a few New Jersey newspapers of his own, as well as dabbling in real estate.

* * *

To many people's minds, the military is something like the ideal bureaucracy. It is supposed to be above partisanship, above fleeting electoral concerns, guided by an almost ancient-seeming code of honor. That's one of the reasons that so many people in the United States were optimistic about the presidency of General Dwight Eisenhower. If plain old Harry Truman hadn't cleaned up the Swamp, maybe the polished man in uniform would do the trick.

Naturally, Ike's administration ended up having its own scandals.

In 1958, Eisenhower's Federal Communications Commission chairman, George C. McConaughey, was forced to resign after a House influence-peddling investigation subcommittee heard testimony that McConaughey had received over a quarter million dollars in bribes for awarding the license that created Pittsburgh TV channel 4.

McConaughey was quickly replaced as FCC chairman by John Doerfer—who in turn had to resign in 1960 after revelations that a friend from whom he'd accepted a boat ride in Florida was really a prominent local broadcasting executive, who had also treated Doerfer to a Bimini vacation and a week of partying on the executive's yacht. It's a reminder of why government issues licenses for things in the first place—they're a great excuse for a lucrative shakedown.

But was the problem isolated to the FCC? Maybe the White House itself was morally spotless? Nope, sorry. A bit earlier, in 1958, Eisenhower's chief of staff, Sherman Adams, was forced to resign over his refusal to answer questions from an investigating subcommittee about the source of an oriental rug and an expensive vicuña wool coat given to his wife. They'd come from Bernard Goldfine, a Boston textile business owner who just happened to be under investigation at the time by the Federal Trade Commission and in need of an ally in Congress. Goldfine, too, refused to answer subcommittee questions and was found in contempt of Congress.

Columnist Jack Anderson—a longtime colleague of Drew Pearson, who'd exposed J. Parnell Thomas's kickback scheme—helped draw attention to the Adams/Goldfine collusion. As Anderson once put it, "The relationship between government and big business thrives in the dark."

What, then, about the presidential administration that has in our time become perhaps the most overly romanticized, the Kennedy administration? Though JFK is now remembered through the rose-colored lens of his family's good looks and the tragedy of his assassination, there's no question that even Camelot was built in the Swamp.

It is often glossed over in today's cursory accounts, but Kennedy was hated by numerous factions during his brief presidency. Even without widespread public knowledge of the drug use and weird sex that reportedly characterized his time in the White House, his military misadventures were enough to earn him serious enemies, often on both sides of a conflict. To the dismay of the Communist North Vietnamese and the growing U.S. counterculture, Kennedy escalated the war in Vietnam—but he didn't stop there. He had a hand in organizing the assassination of the South Vietnamese president, a fellow Catholic, as well, since the South wasn't pressing the war strongly enough to please the U.S. government.

President Kennedy was so infatuated with young, beautiful women, it is a surprise he had time to make so many enemies! "Ask not what your country can do for you, but what you can do for JFK" could have been a corollary to his famous dictum.

Kennedy made an even stranger array of enemies with his bungling of the attempted overthrow of the Castro regime in Cuba in 1962. The Bay of Pigs invasion by exiled Cuban anticommunists was organized with the help of the CIA and was planned—prior to JFK's election—to coincide with the deployment of U.S. air support. Kennedy let the ground invasion proceed but at the eleventh hour balked at providing the air support, leading to the slaughter of the invasion force. Hundreds of CIA assets were lost, arguably the biggest one-day blow the CIA ever suffered.

By the time the Bay of Pigs fiasco was over, Kennedy was hated by pro-Castro Communists, anti-Castro Cuban exiles and their conservative U.S. supporters, and his own CIA. Thanks to the civil rights turmoil and Cold War intrigues of the era, he was also hated by the Klan, the Mob, the FBI, the Soviets, anti-Catholics, and others. That was no way to reassure an often-bigoted nation then still wary about whether having a Catholic president meant having to worry about whether their president might have divided loyalties and take his marching orders from Rome.

That charge was hardly fair, of course. And Kennedy, like most U.S. politicians, might have been better off with a bit more direct moral guidance from some loftier authority. Still, for all his flaws, he does look like a knight compared to the consummate Swamp creature who was his vice president and who rose to the presidency upon JFK's assassination: the amoral operator named Lyndon Johnson.

10. FROM GREAT SOCIETY TO -GATE SOCIETY

When the president does it, that means it is not illegal.
—PRESIDENT RICHARD NIXON

I was eleven years old and in sixth grade when Richard Nixon waved from the steps of his helicopter on August 9, 1974, and his presidency came to a bizarre and rather shocking end. I worried about what this meant for the country. It tugged at my emerging conservative heartstrings. It was a sad exit for a presidency that had begun with law-and-order themes, vowing to oppose the moral chaos of the "counterculture" era. While I might not have fully understood what was going on, I did understand that the president of the United States had done something bad and dishonest. And that alone was both confusing and concerning for me. Hard to fully grasp, actually.

In 1968, Nixon had accepted his party's nomination with the promise to end a troubled period in which "the nation with the greatest tradition of the rule of law is plagued by unprecedented lawlessness." By November 1973, nine months before he left office, he was reduced to assuring Americans during a press conference that "I am not a crook." (What an ironic twist of fate and history.)

Nixon was immersed in party-politics wheeling and dealing long before the Watergate scandal that led to his resignation. In an interview with Randy Dotinga, author Mark Feldstein recounts the events described in his book *Poisoning the Press*, whereby Nixon's desire to have the 1972 Republican convention take place in San Diego may have led to both the Watergate break-in and an assassination threat. The International Telephone and Telegraph Corporation donated a whopping $400,000 to the convention—in return for asking that some antitrust litigation pending against the company be stopped. Columnist Jack Anderson (whom we met in the previous chapter) got his hands on a memo from an ITT lobbyist that outlined the plan, and it even contained the instruction "Please destroy this." Anderson and others widely publicized the brazen memo. While some creatures in Washington lurk in the shadows of the Swamp and deal in hiding, others are bolder and many of them make the mistake of putting their illegal, unethical, or corrupt ways in writing. In hindsight, this type of quid pro quo would be deemed both illegal and unethical on every level. It is shocking that all parties thought they would get away with the scheme.

The scandal didn't end there, though, since the confirmation of the quid pro quo contradicted false testimony given by both John Mitchell, Nixon's attorney general, and Richard Helms, the director of the CIA, attesting that there was nothing fishy about the $400,000. The Nixon White House tried to squash the scandal by spreading the rumor that the lobbyist, Dita Beard, was a lesbian, hoping that would discredit her. In reality, Beard appears to have been a promiscuously heterosexual, hard-drinking, smoking, swearing tough cookie, and ITT may have rewarded her silence, says Feldstein, with a farm of her own in West Virginia.

The Republican Party was embarrassed enough by the ITT donation to move the convention from San Diego to Miami. Nixon

became more paranoid and prone to cover-ups, suggests Feldstein, contributing to his later Watergate mind-set, when Nixon likely approved his team of "plumbers" breaking into the Democratic campaign office at D.C.'s Watergate Hotel for the simple reason that he was by now convinced everyone else was up to no good and the Democrats were probably out to get him somehow. Having convinced himself it was just playing political hardball, not a crime, covering it up followed logically.

If you can't fully blame Nixon for being paranoid after a life in politics, you also can't blame the public for being cynical—and increasingly in the 1970s, they were. A healthy dose of skepticism when dealing with politicians is a useful perspective. There is a common theme throughout these scandalous stories. At some point, before passing the point of no return, many of these scandals could have been fixed, but then people panic, and the cover-up begins. It's always the cover-up that upends these politicians. Remember these words; they will come up again. And again.

It's not as though the 1960s, however, had ended on a note of squeaky-clean government.

Beyond the haze of pot smoke and happy hippie memories was President Lyndon B. Johnson bullying opponents, carrying on extramarital affairs, and lying the United States into greater involvement in the Vietnam War by misrepresenting the circumstances of the Gulf of Tonkin incident, in which a U.S. ship almost certainly fought with mere false readings on its radar but nonetheless inspired a congressional Gulf of Tonkin Resolution, granting LBJ the power to make war on behalf of any Southeast Asian country threatened by "Communist aggression."

Even what is usually depicted by liberals as LBJ's biggest achievement—his array of poverty- and racism-combating "Great Society" programs—was inspired partly by LBJ's cynical private calculations that African Americans, once overwhelmingly Republican, would be inclined to vote for Democrats in gratitude for the next fifty years. Make no mistake: Politicians do very little out of the goodness of their hearts.

And in another reminder that reform and scandal are all too often bundled together in D.C., Senator Thomas Dodd of Connecticut—whose son Christopher's own Senate career would mingle both fishy home loan deals and the role of banking regulation reformer after the 2008 financial crisis—was censured by the Senate in 1967 for financial misconduct. The elder Dodd had a track record of combating misconduct. He'd been an FBI agent and part of the United States' legal team at Nuremberg prosecuting Nazi war crimes. He was also an antigun crusader, though, and that earned him plenty of political enemies interested in digging up dirt on him, if there was any.

Rumors of financial improprieties and alcoholism surrounded him, but what took him down was his transferring of campaign funds to his own accounts for use on personal items unrelated to his Senate campaigns—one of the most common recurring temptations for corrupt politicians. He got a rare censure from the Senate, and he failed in his retaliatory lawsuit against columnist Drew Pearson for inducing former Dodd staffers to reveal documents from Dodd's files about the misappropriation of funds, and for libeling Dodd by publicizing the records.

After that, Dodd was sufficiently damaged goods that in 1970, the Democrats backed a primary opponent against him, who won the primary but lost the general election along with Dodd, who ran as an independent, to liberal Republican Lowell Weicker. A few months later, the defeated and distraught former senator died of a heart attack.

Dodd's son Christopher would go on to become a senator ten years later. At the end of Christopher's own thirty-year Senate career, he helped impose the burdensome and intrusive Dodd-Frank Act on the financial system, increasing firms' reporting requirements and launching a new "consumer protection" bureaucracy. Yet even as he dictated behavior to Wall Street, he was mired in controversy over things like the "friends of Angelo" special-favor mortgage program that Countrywide Financial head Angelo Mozilo was running, in which a few members of Congress participated. Dodd got below-market rates on mortgages for his homes, one in Connecticut and one right in the Swamp, D.C.

Back in the Nixon years, Congress saw a member from New Jersey—Representative Cornelius Gallagher—do two years in prison for tax evasion and his fellow Democrat, California's Richard T. Hanna, sent to prison for a year for taking a $200,000 bribe from a Korean businessman in what came to be nicknamed "Koreagate." As the affixing of the Watergate-inspired -gate suffix to every scandal became part of the American political lexicon, neither the legislative nor executive branch had a monopoly on scandal. We have checks and balances, after all. The judicial branch had a corruption scandal at the highest possible level—the Supreme Court.

Though a mere delay in Supreme Court confirmation hearings is enough to get some people worrying about a constitutional crisis these days, imagine the consternation in May 1969, when a Supreme Court justice had to resign over accusations he'd been bribed. In 1965, Abe Fortas had been appointed by Lyndon Johnson, who also tried nominating Fortas for the position of chief justice in 1968 but was stymied. Protracted hearings dwelled on Fortas's receiving $15,000 for nine speeches at the law school of American University, a fee paid by an array of private companies that might well have business before the Court at some point. When Nixon took office the following year, he seemed to render the issue moot by appointing Warren Burger chief justice—but Fortas's scandals weren't over.

In 1969, it became apparent Fortas had accepted slightly stranger payments starting back in 1966. The family foundation of Wall Street financier Louis Wolfson had agreed to pay Fortas $20,000 a year for the rest of his life (and then to pay Fortas's widow) for unspecified legal advice. And since Wolfson was under investigation for securities violations, investigators suspected Fortas's job was to help Wolfson escape punishment—possibly even via a presidential pardon if necessary. On top of all that, J. Edgar Hoover at the FBI had turned against Fortas, suspecting him (and possibly other judges) of involvement in a tax-dodging scheme.

In the end, though, what persuaded Fortas to resign, he claimed, was his desire to shift the spotlight of attention off the Supreme Court for the sake of his fellow justice William O. Douglas, who was also under investigation—and nearly impeached at the urging of future president Gerald Ford—for receiving money from a well-connected family foundation.

When people talk about the sanctity and independence of the judiciary, they express a noble ideal, but if they think they're describing the courts as they operate in the real world, they must be suffering from historical amnesia.

Multiple members of Congress were convicted of tax evasion and kickbacks in the early '70s, but no scandal cast a darker shadow and had a bigger impact on the public psyche than the Watergate break-in and Nixon's attempt to cover it up. His CREEP group (Committee for the Re-Election of the President) also operated a slush fund that distributed nearly a million dollars to, among other people, Representative William Oswald Mills, Republican of Maryland—who committed suicide within a week after his payment was revealed.

Mills shot himself in the chest, leaving behind several pessimistic suicide notes—but ironically, he might have survived a legal inquiry. Taking the CREEP money was sleazy but not obviously illegal, not under the campaign finance laws of the day. Given how rare it is these days for a politician's career to be ended by any scandal—instead of a phony apology being issued at a press conference and a new phase of the career beginning—it's hard for most of us today to imagine a politician choosing to "take the honorable way out."

CREEP's less damaging but still creepy political dirty tricks included stunts like forging a letter from Democratic presidential front-runner Edmund Muskie during the New Hampshire primary, which made it appear Muskie disparaged the state's French-Canadian-descended population as "Canucks." A CREEP operative pleaded guilty to forging documents to embarrass Democrats.

The Nixon years left behind literal bodies as well as the corpses of numerous political careers. Nixon's first vice president, Spiro Agnew, was convicted of tax fraud in a bribery and extortion case and resigned a few months after the Mills suicide. Agnew was the first vice president to resign since John Calhoun. It was a sorry end for a former Maryland governor who was briefly beloved by conservatives for insulting antiwar activists and the press with descriptions like "nattering nabobs of negativism." A year before Agnew's resignation, Nixon and his closest advisors were already dreaming of luring Agnew off the Republican ticket for 1972 by persuading conservatives to buy a TV network and offer Agnew the chance to run it—or by asking Bob Hope to make him his business partner.

Nixon's CIA director, Richard Helms, was convicted of misleading Congress about assassination attempts in Cuba—but he was law-abiding enough to turn down White House chief of staff H. R. Haldeman's request for $1 million to pay the Watergate burglars to keep silent after their arrests. If such a payment were ever discovered by the public, feared Helms, it could spell the end of the agency.

* * *

Nixon was also one of about a half-dozen presidents known to have used the IRS as a political weapon—in Nixon's case against everyone from protestors to reporters. "Are we going after their tax returns? You know what I mean? There's a lot of gold in them there hills," Nixon told advisor John Ehrlichman. Politicians' temptation to abuse the power of the IRS continues right down to the present, of course.

In early 2017, the IRS claimed it has suddenly found nearly seven thousand documents related to the targeting of conservative and Tea Party groups for extra scrutiny five years earlier, at exactly the time such groups might have presented a threat to the presidential re-election prospects of Barack Obama. Two years prior, the Department of Justice declined to file charges against Lois Lerner, who had been in charge of the IRS division examining nonprofit groups at the time of the biased reviews. Having resigned and partially apologized in 2013, it's unlikely she'll be packed off to jail now no matter what turns up in any formerly "lost" emails.

But the Department of Justice has not always been so feckless in its pursuit of IRS wrongdoing.

The year 1950 also saw the Department of Justice investigating the IRS, but in that case, it led to the firing or resignation of 166 IRS employees, consequences that never seem to happen when bad government behavior is brought to light today. The punishment of the IRS staffers back then is made all the more remarkable by the fact that IRS wrongdoing in those days was even more likely to have presidential fingerprints on it than under today's rules. In the first half of the twentieth century, presidents began to wield the power to appoint regional tax collectors, often treating the positions as patronage jobs for their cronies. In 1950, rumors began to circulate that well-connected citizens were able to bribe IRS employees to overlook irregularities. Republican senator John J. Williams of Delaware called for an investigation.

Unfortunately, the investigation ended up fighting itself, as Attorney General Howard McGrath and special assistant Newbold Morris, who was tasked with investigating public corruption, argued about how broad the investigation should be. Unable to rein in Morris, who wanted to see McGrath's personal records, McGrath fired him but later resigned himself, dissatisfied with the progress of the investigation. The efforts were not in vain, though. Numerous prosecutions and firings resulted, including the dismissal of the St. Louis district tax collection head, James Finnegan, who was known to be a close friend of President Harry Truman. Truman has a reputation today for being a stand-up guy, but his presidency, too, ended with multiple investigations and accusations of corruption. Most do.

Even the numerous prosecutions, however, were not enough to restore public trust in the IRS. Arguably, it has never recovered, but the Truman-era scandal did inspire institutional reforms, including replacing presidential patronage positions with career bureaucrats. In the Swamp, sometimes bureaucracy is an improvement.

Corruption can get you far in D.C., but it's not often that it's captured on video with easy-to-comprehend suitcases full of cash and fake Arab sheiks. So it was in the late '70s and early '80s, in one of several cases in which authorities managed to catch the Swamp creatures doing their dirty work, in the so-called Abscam sting.

It began when the FBI ensnared a talented con man named Mel Weinberg, who had been getting suckers to front him large amounts of money so that he could process their applications to a company handling the offshoring of finances. But there was no real, functioning company, so all the applications went nowhere, and Weinberg pocketed all the fronted money. As recounted by *Inside Jersey* magazine and fictionalized in the movie *American Hustle*, the FBI decided that rather than send Weinberg to prison, it could use his talents as a scammer to catch other con artists. The flamboyant, cigar-smoking Weinberg was delighted to help out—and to earn commissions from the FBI for each of his fellow crooks he ensnared.

Then the FBI decided to aim higher, or rather lower, into the Swamp, for targets. First ensnaring New Jersey state senator Angelo Errichetti, getting him to take money purportedly to fix permits for Weinberg with the casino commission in Atlantic City, the FBI now had under their thumb a crook big enough to set up meetings with other high-profile targets, including ones from D.C., who were willing to take cash—unwittingly doing so on hidden camera—and reveal just how corrupt they were. "I'll give you Atlantic City," Errichetti said on the resulting sting videos. "Without me, you do nothing." But soon he was giving the FBI other corrupt politicians instead.

The physical mechanics of the stings were simple enough: meetings set up with Weinberg or Errichetti leading to paper bags of thousands of dollars in cash exiting with the target politicians after they promised favors, with meetings taking place on yachts, on private jets, in hotels, in limos, and at parties, as *Inside Jersey* recounts. To create plausible bribers big enough to lure the D.C. politicians required conjuring up fictional Arab sheiks with millions to spend, roles that were played by actors.

One of the ensnared, bribe-taking congressman Michael "Ozzie" Myers—a Pennsylvania Democrat and former longshoreman with a propensity for profanity and violence—memorably told one of the sting participants, "I'm gonna tell you something real simple and short: Money talks in this business and bullshit walks. And it works the same way down in Washington." With that, he took an envelope full of $50,000 in hundred-dollar bills and earned himself three years in prison.

This 1980 scandal was a low point for Americans' faith in their political institutions at the tail end of the dispiriting and disillusioning 1970s. They were tired of the revelations of corruption, tired of the scandals. They had not been appeased by Democratic and born-again Christian president Jimmy Carter's homespun efforts to bring a tone of moral humility to the office (humility that turned out to be well deserved, given his inability to cope with domestic and foreign-policy crises). Americans were ready for someone bringing a message of old-time morals and national renewal.

They got it in the form of 1980 Republican candidate Ronald Reagan, who did not so much campaign against Carter as against government itself—and thus the Swamp. Whether even he managed to drain it much remains debatable.

11. A REPUBLICAN SOAK IN THE SWAMP

Government is not the solution to our problem; government is the problem.

—RONALD REAGAN

Ronald Reagan remains a great inspiration to conservatives. But there's only so much even a president can do to combat the Swamp.

The dominant conservative philosophy at the time, as represented by institutions such as the magazine *National Review*, was a blend of optimistic free-market principles and Judeo-Christian morals, both seen as reining in an out-of-control big government—aside from a big boost in defense spending to combat the Soviet Union during the final decade of its existence.

Shrinking government and cleaning up Washington should go hand in hand. As Reagan put it in one of his radio addresses, "I'm talking about reducing waste, fraud, abuse, and mismanagement in government—problems that for too long were permitted to grow and spread like an unchecked cancer, plundering your pocketbooks, and hindering government's ability to provide essential public services in an efficient and timely manner."

Sounds fantastic. Sign me up. But for every seemingly ridiculous item in the budget, there were defenders. In the late '70s and the 1980s, Senator William Proxmire, Democrat of Wisconsin, gave out a Golden Fleece Award to the most absurd examples of government spending he could find—things like a National Institutes of Health study of Peruvian brothels, a $4 million Postal Service push encouraging Americans to write letters, and $100,000 to the National Science Foundation to see whether sunfish were more aggressive when drinking gin or tequila. If Proxmire's award helped shine a light on waste, it seemed that both parties were on the verge of getting the idea and inching away from ever-ballooning government and its waste of taxpayers' dollars. More recently, Senator Rand Paul has taken on the mantle of highlighting egregious government waste. In a recent speech, Senator Paul highlighted the National Institutes of Health spending almost $200,000 on a study to determine if Japanese quail are more or less sexually promiscuous when high on cocaine! Believe me, you can't make this stuff up!

But even "seismic" shifts in political thinking usually aren't as big as the hype surrounding them. The government was no smaller when Reagan left office than when he entered. He had merely slowed its growth, though that was a heroic achievement—and he stared down the even bigger-government philosophy, armed with nukes overseas, in the form of the Soviet Union. Still, Democrats retained control of the House throughout Reagan's presidency, as they had since the middle of Eisenhower's first term, in the 1950s, and as they would until the 1994 "Gingrich Revolution" that brought the Republicans control of both houses of Congress. The Democrats railed against Reagan's defense increases, but their main priority was protecting domestic spending programs, and they largely succeeded.

From the perspective of someone hoping to see government shrink, the Republicans and Democrats began to look like a codependent relationship, or worse, a pair of cooperating con artists: One would look the other way while the other spent wildly at home, then the other one would look away while the first spent wildly overseas—that is, on increased military projects.

For any partisan group, the issues about which they feel most passionate can easily become moral blind spots. I'm sure most Democrats honestly wish antipoverty programs worked well, so they're just not going to be as critical of that "waste, fraud, and abuse" Reagan mentioned when it happens in the programs they love as they are of the military projects in which they have less interest.

Similarly, the halo of duty and honor that rightly surrounds the military can distract patriotic conservatives from reckless and even illegal spending on military and espionage projects, as surely as our love of law and order can sometimes make us slow to acknowledge the few bad apples that might be present.

The Iran-Contra scandal was the quintessential conservative military/espionage scandal. It began, really, with Reagan's admirable frustration at not being able to do more to help the cause of democracy in Nicaragua. Creating something like a twentieth-century version of the Monroe Doctrine, Reagan was as strongly opposed to Communism making inroads in Central America as John F. Kennedy had been to Khrushchev putting missiles in Cuba. But scandal had already plagued efforts to help the Nicaraguan anticommunist forces, with Democrats in Congress objecting to civilian deaths and revelations of terrorist tactics by the Nicaraguan Contra forces who were resisting the Communist government run by Daniel Ortega.

Congress passed multiple laws, including the 1982 Boland Amendment, expressly forbidding any U.S. military aid to Nicaragua. To Reagan—and to his conservative boosters at places like *National Review*—the Contras remained something bigger and more important than their record of wins, losses, or war crimes. The

Contras were freedom fighters and had developed a moral glow explicitly likened by some conservatives at the time to that surrounding our own nation's Founding Fathers.

Of course, as we learned earlier, even the Founding Fathers were far from perfect. An illegal operation to fund foreign paramilitary fighters stood a good chance of becoming far from perfect, in hindsight.

Reagan turned for advice to his director of the CIA, William Casey. How much the president knew and when he knew it would become a source of debate for journalists, historians, and investigatory congressional committees that has filled volumes all by itself. But it appears Casey, at least, was aware that a Marine lieutenant colonel assigned to the National Security Council, Oliver North, would get around Congress's block on direct governmental aid to the Contras through a three-step scheme that in retrospect looks like something that should have been avoided.

If Reagan and the U.S. military couldn't aid the Contras directly—something that chafed at Reagan as a constraint on his presidential authority over the military and as an abandonment of allies—then under the scheme North oversaw, money from missile sales to the new radical Muslim government of Iran would flow to the then-U.S.-allied government of President Manuel Noriega in Panama, and Noriega would get aid to the nearby Nicaraguan rebels.

What could possibly go wrong?

By the time the scandal was over, Reagan's reputation as a tough hawk would, of strategic necessity, be replaced by the claim that he was a hands-off president—providing a romantic guiding vision for foreign policy decisions but not necessarily steeped in the details, which he left to the CIA and down-and-dirty operatives like North (a romantic visionary in his own right who toured conservative and industry events, speaking on behalf of the Contra cause in hopes of drumming up support that would further alleviate the need for any U.S. government funds).

North would become a convicted felon, and several other members of the Reagan administration would be charged with crimes for their roles in covering up the operation.

In a sense, the Iran-Contra scandal did not end until Reagan's vice president, George H. W. Bush, did what Reagan could not without creating still more scandal and pardoned several of the Iran-Contra participants just before Bush ended his own single term as president. Bush pardoned six people tied to the Iran-Contra scandal on his final Christmas Eve in office in 1992, including former secretary of defense Caspar Weinberger, former national security advisor Robert McFarlane, and State Department official Elliott Abrams. North got a community service sentence, though North's original conviction was later overturned with the help of the American Civil Liberties Union, a group that's sometimes friendly with today's libertarians but was often a rhetorical punching bag for the Reagan-era right.

Fawn Hall, North's secretary, was granted immunity from prosecution in exchange for testimony against North, whom she had so vigorously defended during the initial Iran-Contra hearings that dominated TV news coverage in 1987.

Scandals come in different sizes. It's not always obvious which ones should worry us most. Is it the pure venality of petty graft? The callousness of a married politician's torrid affair? Is it the minor deviations from law that have a huge impact on policy or the economy through the tweaking of regulations?

Though George H. W. Bush's presidency would see members of Congress convicted in court or denounced by the Senate for bribery, tax fraud, and financial crimes—as in prior decades of Swamp life—one reason the Iran-Contra scandal continued to echo was that it hinted at a whole world of potential law-breaking taking place deep, deep below the surface of the Swamp, concealed not just by the usual clumsy Congress members' lies and staffers' selective losing of documents but also by the noblest-sounding national security rationales.

What conservative didn't want to fight Communism, especially right on our doorstep in the Americas?

But you can't rein in government in the long run, at least not with consistency—not with adherence to principle—if you're defying Congress and the law to do it, all while keeping secrets from the American people. It's hard enough tracing the envelopes of cash and the artfully named special subsidies to select industries that make up the normal day-to-day business of the Swamp. How does one really keep track of wrongdoing in the covert world, whether as a citizen or a journalist? How does one trace the connections between people who operate in the shadows with legal authority, extralegal authority, or simply the zeal to act without authorization? The Cold War required secrecy and sometimes dubious methods, but even fighting Communism should not be an excuse for corruption.

These concerns are one of many reasons to see Trump's potential role as reformer as encouraging. He claims to be on good terms with the intelligence community that serves him, but we can see he distrusts them a bit, and a little bit of distrust can make one a better watchdog. The trappings of the White House can easily confuse and disorient an honest person. Before you know it, the Swamp sucks you in and you're part of the problem, part of the establishment, and just as filthy as the people you campaigned against in the previous election. Make no mistake—clean, naive, and bushy-tailed politicians quickly get swallowed and spit back out by the monsters that lurk in Washington's Swamp. It is good for them to be suspicious of it.

* * *

What kept Iran-Contra from bubbling up out of the Swamp into a broader distrust of government—or a broader distrust of our military and espionage apparatus among conservatives—was the fact that in 1989, eleven months after Reagan left office, European Communism utterly collapsed, thanks in no small part to Reagan's efforts in keeping the military and moral pressure on them—and thanks, of course, to the laws of economics, which dictate that all socialist projects will end in disaster eventually. Reagan today stands as one of the best presidents in our entire history, and despite the Swamp creatures that surrounded him, he was able to persevere.

George H. W. Bush, who had been CIA director himself a few years before becoming Reagan's vice presidential running mate, may have seen an opportunity to clean house as the Cold War ended, and the very same week that the Berlin Wall was being breached by elated Germans, marking the end to one of the greatest tyrannies humanity has ever known, Bush was invading Panama. Some of our troops stationed there had been assaulted by the locals, and there was ample evidence of Noriega's involvement in the drug trade—but was that sufficient reason for the invasion?

It did have the positive side effect, from certain scandal participants' perspective, of putting one last player in their three-sided arms-money-rebels scheme in prison, far from the levers of political power, far from routine press inquiries, far from further investigator questions, save for the most narrowly planned of purposes.

Did taking down Noriega mean one of the most gruesome of the Swamp's distant cousins was rightly taken out of the picture and brought to justice? Or did it mean that a very embarrassing living reminder of other Swamp creatures' misdeeds was safely out of the picture? Politicians themselves often have mixed motives and they—and we—may not know the precise reasons for their actions.

12. CONTRACT WITH AMERICA, CONTACT WITH AN INTERN

As president, I will take steps to ban the box, so former presidents won't have to declare their criminal history at the very start of the hiring process.
—HILLARY CLINTON, MISSPEAKING ABOUT FELONS
ON THE CAMPAIGN TRAIL

So numerous are the scandals in the Swamp that sometimes one collides with another. Most Americans probably recall President Bill Clinton having an affair with White House intern Monica Lewinsky—and many recall that Bill was impeached. Fewer likely recall that there was nothing about the affair itself that was illegal, though it obviously raised recurring moral questions about Bill.

Bill Clinton was impeached for lying to a grand jury about the Lewinsky affair while he was being questioned about the sexual harassment claims of Paula Jones.

In fact, liberals should have been high-fiving each other when national attention shifted away from Jones's serious accusations of workplace harassment and further shifted away from the issue of perjury before a grand jury to the lesser question of whether Bill and Lewinsky had a consensual sexual relationship. Suddenly, in 1998, our national standards for gauging scandal were ratcheted downward, as though any legal matter that touched upon sex was only a matter of sex.

During grand jury questioning on a range of alleged political and financial misdeeds, what should have been a debate over a pattern of sexual harassment and even sexual assault claims against Bill, and a debate over the proper legal and constitutional consequences for presidential perjury, became instead a lascivious national conversation about whether Lewinsky was a badly behaved woman and whether Hillary Clinton was in pain about the state of her marriage.

The likely truth is that both Clintons were in pain—about the threat to their political agenda and to the prospects for their anointed successor, Vice President Al Gore, being able to win the 2000 election and carry on their political legacy. As for the marriage, it is likely Hillary had long since accepted a deal based as much on political power and personal self-indulgence as on any traditional notions of fidelity. Bill's philandering had been widely rumored and seemingly prolific since back in his Arkansas days.

It was during that time, on May 8, 1991, that Bill, according to Jones, invited her to his room in Little Rock's Excelsior Hotel. Then twenty-four years old, Jones was probably both impressed and intimidated by Bill. Imagine being lavished with that type of attention as you walk into a posh hotel with such a prominent politician. He was, and remains, notoriously charming—often likened to Elvis with his chubby good looks and confident swagger. But he was also her boss. That would have made things more than a little awkward for her when, she alleges, Bill unceremoniously took off his pants and asked her to perform oral sex on him—revealing a unique misshapen attribute that would be recalled by more than one of Bill's victims and/or liaisons.

Jones said no to Bill's suggestion. The supremely entitled young governor probably regarded it as impertinence on her part. But there would be other women. There always were.

Ironically, Jones says what later convinced her to sue was a 1993 article in *The American Spectator* about Bill's history of sexual misbehavior by David Brock, who just a few years later would break with conservatism and become one of the Clintons' most ardent defenders, informally running much of the pro-Clinton media machine during Hillary's 2016 presidential run and fiercely combating rumors, both founded and unfounded, about the Clintons' misdeeds.

Back in 1997, Bill tried having his lawyers argue before the Supreme Court that he should not be tried for wrongs committed prior to becoming president and that Jones's suit should be dismissed. The Supreme Court, unanimously, was unpersuaded. Bill maintained his innocence—but forked over $850,000 as a settlement to Jones to end the matter in November 1998.

The following month, faced with testimony and recordings from Lewinsky confidante and fellow White House employee Linda Tripp that suggested Lewinsky had knowingly lied to protect her president, the House of Representatives voted on Ken Starr's evidence that Bill Clinton had committed perjury about the relationship, no mere political sin but an arguable "high crime or misdemeanor" warranting removal from office. Though both the House and Senate were dominated by Republicans, the charges, though voted sufficient for removal in the House in December, were not reaffirmed by the Senate in February, which was not widely regarded as a surprise. Clinton, then, was impeached but not convicted and remained in office.

Furthermore, the Republicans, who had hoped to gain seats in the 1998 midterm elections—seemingly a safe bet for the opposing party late in a presidential administration, especially with that president suffering an embarrassing scandal—instead lost three seats in the House, a humiliation that contributed to Newt Gingrich exiting the speakership and choosing not to run for reelection to his seat in Congress. Bill Clinton, a master of political jujitsu, successfully turned the scandal in many Americans' minds into evidence of Republican prudery instead of his own criminality.

Bill's credibility never fully recovered, though. The memory of him hairsplittingly telling the grand jury things like "It depends on what the meaning of the word *is* is" when asked if there was a sexual relationship between him and Lewinsky was too vivid to forget.

The most famous piece of physical evidence from the scandal, Monica Lewinsky's blue dress, on which she attested there was "DNA" from Clinton left over from one of their encounters, was last known to be in Lewinsky's possession, though there was speculation at one point that the Smithsonian might buy it, and a Las Vegas sex museum offered $1 million for it. What sex museum wouldn't want an artifact tied to only the second presidential impeachment in history?

The Clintons' time in the White House—and before that, the governor's mansion in Arkansas—left us with more than one scandal, though. The Clintons are a sort of swamp unto themselves, producing numerous -*gate* controversies.

I noted earlier Hillary's uncanny "good luck" in trading cattle futures, a truly remarkable performance by a novice in a volatile market, which could be happy coincidence—or not.

Arkansas state troopers claimed they were often pressured into facilitating and covering up Bill's numerous sexual liaisons.

Several Clinton associates went to prison over the Clintons' shady Whitewater Development Corporation land deal, in which Susan McDougal secured an illegal $300,000 loan in the 1980s from judge and banker David Hale, who later alleged the Clintons had pressured him into making the loan. As president, Bill would pardon McDougal.

The Whitewater investigation led to Clinton advisor and U.S. associate attorney general Webb Hubbell, who had been a mayor, state supreme court chief justice, and lawyer back in Arkansas, serving over a year and a half in jail for tax fraud and wire fraud.

While friends and business partners of the Clintons go to jail, the Clintons themselves always somehow stay one step ahead of investigators. So it was when Hillary's own records of dealing with Susan McDougal's husband, Jim, in her days at Arkansas's Rose Law Firm went missing in the mid-'90s at exactly the time investigators were looking for them to see how deep the Clintons' involvement in the McDougal land deals was. Immediately *after* the investigation was closed, the files were found by Hillary's assistant Carolyn Huber, who claimed the files must have been unwittingly removed from Hillary's book room for some reason six months earlier.

Perhaps Hillary's former Rose Law Firm colleague Vince Foster knew something that troubled him about Clinton criminality, since he committed suicide while serving at the White House and left behind a note denouncing D.C. as a place where people destroy each other. Conspiracy theorists still claim the Clintons had something to do with Vince Foster's death, though no charges were ever brought in the case.

Upon entering the White House, the Clintons fired the White House travel staff and inserted their own business cronies in their place, in what came to be known as Travelgate.

Ironically, given Hillary's early days as a lawyer investigating Nixon's Watergate misdeeds, the Clintons were downright Nixonian in using the federal bureaucracy against their foes, accessing FBI files to look for damaging information.

In another case of one Clinton scandal leading to another, Kathleen Willey was called upon to testify in the Paula Jones suit about her own alleged assault by Bill, and when Bill testified to investigators in 1998, denying sexual contact with Willey, he admitted to a consensual sexual relationship lasting over a decade with *Penthouse* model Gennifer Flowers. Bill's sex life really hasn't been subtle.

Charlie Trie, Taiwanese immigrant and Little Rock, Arkansas, restaurateur, was one of many people convicted of steering Chinese donations toward the Democratic National Committee and Clinton associates.

The use of intermediates to raise otherwise illegal foreign funds, including Chinese government–linked funds, for U.S. campaign purposes would haunt Al Gore during his own 2000 presidential run, making him appear a poor messenger for reforming D.C. and campaign finance rules after the revelation of his own legally suspect fund-raising from Buddhist temples at which large amounts of foreign money flowed, some of which had to be given back after an investigation.

The Clintons exited the White House on a sleazy note even by the standards of many of their liberal defenders, pardoning donors and cronies with little apparent regard for justice—even pardoning one international fugitive from justice. Bill also seems to have secured burial in Arlington Cemetery for one donor who hadn't served in the military.

Between Bill's time in the Oval Office with interns in blue dresses and Hillary's as secretary of state under Obama, the Clinton Foundation appeared to serve as an unofficial, private version of the State Department, facilitating business deals and NGO partnerships around the world—and usually getting the Clintons a big cut in the process. Both Clintons also received huge speaking fees from Wall Street firms and others during that time, an easy way to curry favor with the politically well connected if that were one's motive.

Incredibly, even during Hillary's time at the State Department, the foundation would continue raking in big bucks from countries with an interest in changes in U.S. policy—including from Russia, a country whose ties to the Trump administration we keep hearing about, but who managed to buy about a fifth of the U.S. supply of uranium on Obama's watch at the same time Russian banks were facilitating massive donations to the Clinton Foundation, without generating much, if any, outrage from Clinton supporters.

But then, the Clintons have always taken a rather lax attitude toward sharing with foreign regimes, as when Bill eased rules on U.S. firms sharing missile technology with China. It all greases the wheels of an international mercantilist machine—as long as no fighting breaks out.

Tragically, Hillary and others at the State Department appear to have taken a similarly lackadaisical attitude toward security at the State Department's Benghazi, Libya, compound, where local Islamist militia members were entrusted with security, providing little help during an attack on September 11, 2012, that killed, among others, U.S. ambassador Chris Stevens. Hillary had a lot riding on the pretense that the situation in Libya was stable, including a report of potential future business dealings with which she and her advisor Sidney Blumenthal were connected.

Money, more than ideology or any covert religious sympathies, likely explains the Clintons' tolerance for Saudi wrongdoing.

The Saudis are significant donors to most recent presidents' official libraries, among other things. If that makes America a little more likely to look the other way when the Saudis fund terrorism, well, small price to pay.

Throughout the Clinton era, there was a common perception that Bill and Hillary loved money. They loved it so much, they were willing to do almost anything to amass more and more of it. In fact, when in 2014 Hillary declared that she and Bill were "broke" when they left the White House, much of the Clinton credibility was lost forever. That was of little consequence, because within a few years, the Clintons' net worth was estimated at over $100 million. The loss of credibility finally came back to haunt Hillary when she ran for president in 2016.

America might almost have forgotten about the Clintons' habitual deceit and sleazy dealing—might have thought of them as embodiments of '90s peace and prosperity—had Hillary not made the mistake of running for president (a second time) in 2016, against a force of nature known as Donald Trump. No present political family exudes a stronger stench from the Swamp than the Clintons.

13. PATH OUT OF THE SWAMP: LIMIT TERMS, LIMIT LOBBYING

Now is the time when men work quietly in the fields and women weep softly in the kitchen; the legislature is in session and no man's property is safe.

—DANIEL WEBSTER

Donald Trump's victory in the presidential election of 2016 would spare the nation a return to rule by the Clintons—but not before we lived through two other presidencies with scandals of their own in the interim.

George W. Bush mass-fired seven U.S. attorneys he had himself appointed—sparking mass resignations among his staff to avoid testifying on the matter, with no clear explanation for their firing ever emerging.

Barack Obama dissembled about Benghazi, the Fast and Furious gunrunning program, IRS targeting of Tea Party groups, and bogus subsidies like those to the bankrupt Solyndra solar panel company (under the guise of creating a cleaner and more regulated—yet miraculously also more profitable—"green economy").

Neither right nor left seems to have satisfied the public's craving for a government that serves average citizens, a government that resists turning into a secretive, favor-granting machine. So, after decades of watching control of the Swamp lurch back and forth between two parties that were opposites on things that don't matter and all too similar on the things that do—like piling more spending on top of a $20 trillion federal debt—the voters decided to punt to a different option.

It was a risky move. All the experts said it was the wrong one. The voters somehow eliminated establishment Republicans like Jeb Bush in the 2016 primary, then eliminated the ultimate establishment Democrat in the general election in the person of Hillary Clinton. Donald Trump was a paradox but one the voters found somehow compelling. He came from Democrat-dominated New York City. He violated rules of Republican orthodoxy on trade and the Iraq War, flirted with conspiracy theory and lewdness—yet his brazen unwillingness to bend the knee, to flatter the press, to play by the usual rules, spoke to the public's deep longing to be rid of the usual gang of idiots.

He called the Swamp inhabitants "stupid," and you weren't supposed to do that—yet they are. And he did. And he got away with it. And he kept getting away with it right through the November 2016 election, even with the nation's best prognosticators giving him a scientifically validated 98 percent chance of losing.

And if he kneecapped the usual sources of conservative legitimacy—*National Review* called him a "witless ape," but it didn't slow him down—he did even worse to the left, making jokes about sex, age, nationality, and every other category of ordinary human life the left has declared off-limits for discussion for decades, driving the liberal establishment almost literally insane. Their frenzy only increased when he had the audacity to win. This wasn't supposed to happen.

It's happening around the world, though, as people wake up to the fact that the elite have been serving their own needs, not the needs of the public they flatter and pretend to feel so deeply about. The results of elite corruption are becoming increasingly obvious. Even as Trump's victory is interpreted as a sign of a populist uprising in the United States, an array of scandals in Europe—not just the failure of governments to cope with a surge in Muslim migrants but financial and legal controversies as well—have contributed to the populist and right-wing groundswells in elections there, which, going forward, may resemble the change that reached the United States in 2016.

A global uprising against political corruption would render nonsensical the left's charge that Trump is merely an isolationist and nationalist out of touch with the wider world. The decades-long mantra of the international left that the United States is a renegade "cowboy" nation sounds hollow when their own nations begin replacing that mantra with a populist rebel yell. A 2017 study by the group Transparency International suggests that government corruption around the world has been increasing in recent years, after a prior post–Cold War period of diminishment, and that some 85 percent of humanity now lives under what are arguably corrupt governments. Eighty-five percent!

But then, to some degree, there will always be corruption when a few people get to make the decisions and spend money in the name of the rest of the population. All government inhabits a moral Swamp. For America, the question is, how deep is our Swamp? And exactly how does one go about draining the Swamp? That's a tricky question since there are Swamp creatures lurking in every corridor of every floor of every building in D.C.

Even if you agree with this dire assessment, though, you may be left wondering, what can we do? What should Trump do? In these final chapters of this book, I outline a few suggestions, consistent with the thrust of his antiestablishment agenda—and I recommend

some actionable steps President Trump should take in order to *drain
the Swamp.*

First, I would say to Trump: Stick to your business instincts. They
will not fail you.

Liberals and conservatives alike make the mistake of entering the
Swamp and immediately adjusting (or more likely abandoning) their
principles to the business-as-usual habits of the Swamp, instead of
making the Swamp creatures adhere to principle. Populism may be
more a gut instinct rather than a clear policy agenda—but it's that
instinct that warns us the elite are playing a game rigged for their
own benefit, rigged against the rest of us.

That rigging can take the form of subsidies, regulations, and court
decisions that please the well connected but do little for the taxpayers whose hard work keeps the Swamp moist and vibrant. A variety of
populist figures from right and left have expressed that worry, from
Pat Buchanan and Ross Perot in the 1990s (both friendly with the
Reform Party, which at one point encouraged an earlier Trump
run for president) to Bernie Sanders at his best moments in his 2016
run. He was a hopeless old Socialist who would have made D.C.
even more powerful and intrusive and utterly tanked the economy—
but if you get steamrollered by a corrupt Democratic National
Committee that's completely in the tank for Hillary Clinton, you're
bound to gain a little wisdom about how the system serves those who
are already in charge.

How, then, to navigate the Swamp without becoming a part of
it? Staying true to the commonsense principles that make business
work, principles lacking in government, would be a great start.
Trump's son-in-law, publisher and real estate developer Jared
Kushner, put it well when he was interviewed about an initiative
designed to research reform suggestions for potential use by Trump

and his administration: "The government should be run like a great American company. Our hope is that we can achieve successes and efficiencies for our customers, who are the citizens."

Now that one line is exactly the reason I supported Donald Trump for president since he announced that first day in June 2015—eighteen months before the election. That single thought—a businessman running the country for the customers (we American citizens) is why I stayed true to that candidate throughout a very tumultuous election.

Naturally, the left doesn't like that sort of talk. To them, it sounds like an autocratic boss calling all the shots and a frightened staff of 330 million people jumping to obey. But it's not some vague bossiness that government needs to learn from the private sector—it's basics like weighing costs and benefits, seeking competitive bids, carefully accounting for inventory, looking for returns on investment (not just the total amount spent, as if that equals the total amount of good done), and above all phasing out old programs when better methods are available.

The left always makes budget cuts and the phasing out of programs sound cruel, but remember, that's our money those programs are wasting—money that you and I, and lots of other people, could be using to educate our kids or treat our illnesses or fix up our homes. It's crazy to talk about government as if its main purpose should be keeping the nearly three million people who work for it happy. Let some of them find better, more productive jobs in the private sector instead of hiding in a cubicle at the Department of Transportation and hoping no one remembers they're there or asks them what their job is.

White House budget director Mick Mulvaney said the first proposed Trump budget would likely result in layoffs within the federal workforce and, in an interview, expressed it in a way that was music to my ears: "You can't drain the swamp and leave all the people in it." Amen.

Treat the Oval Office as if it were a boardroom, Mr. President, and demand some results.

Second, if Congress spends its time engaged in the unproductive business of creating legislation (most of which will just impose new costs and new restrictions on the economy), why not reduce the number of days Congress is in session each year?

That way, they do less damage and stick to the most important, high-priority legislative business when Congress is in session. The Founding Fathers would have approved. They wanted people to join the legislature and then return to private life to live under the laws they had created, not secure a cushy gig in Congress and then stay there for life, which is the apparent goal of virtually every representative and senator nowadays.

They almost never leave unless they get too old to remain, lose an election, resign amid a scandal (like the ones described in this book), die, or get appointed to some other position such as ambassador. It's very rare that any of them just decide to go be more productive in another sector of society. Even when they leave to "pursue opportunities in the private sector," the odds are it's not a purely free-market activity but instead some sort of public-private project that uses their former political connections and is covered in Swamp slime.

Turn members of Congress back into nearly normal citizens.

In addition to limiting how long Congress is in session each year, of course, there's the long-standing suggestion that we limit the number of terms any member can remain in Congress.

The longer members stay, the more accustomed they get to the

ways of the Swamp. The more they forget they ever had lives before being Swamp creatures. Voters more often than not vote for
the names they recognize on the ballot, so an incumbent almost
always has a huge advantage over a challenger. Over 90 percent
of the time, the incumbent wins in a congressional election. One of
the reasons voters are so easily lulled into thinking the incumbent,
especially the long-term incumbent, must be better than an opponent is that the long-term incumbent can usually point to a long
record of legislative "achievement."

But not all legislation is good.

That same "record of achievement" the typical incumbent points
to is the sediment of onerous rules and regulations (about which,
more next chapter) that tilt the playing field in favor of the establishment and its cronies. As citizens, we can vote for the candidates
of our choice while also recognizing it's good to put a limit on how
many times those candidates, no matter how popular, can run. We
apply that logic to presidents and to governors. Or at least, by tradition the presidents applied the "two terms" rule to themselves,
starting with George Washington, who was eager to show that
in America, unlike in the monarchies back in the Old World, the
executive can peacefully exit government after a short time, without
dying.

When Franklin Roosevelt broke with that tradition (and so many
others, as when he tried to expand the number of justices on the
Supreme Court to give himself more judicial branch allies), Congress responded by making explicit what had been only implicit.
In 1947, just two years after FDR's death in office, Congress passed
the Twenty-Second Amendment to the Constitution (ratified in
1951), limiting a president to two terms.

If it's healthy for our democracy to limit the terms of presidents
and governors, there's no reason we can't limit the terms of members of Congress.

Or rather, there wouldn't be if a constitutional amendment were passed adding term limits to the qualifications for senator and representative spelled out in Article I, Sections 2 and 3 of the Constitution. There was a fast-growing movement in the early 1990s to legislate such term limits at the national level, but when it appeared that effort would not succeed, libertarian and conservative activists quickly launched initiatives on a state-by-state basis to limit each states' congressional delegation's terms. That clever tactic was shot down by the Supreme Court in 1995 on Article I grounds.

This was followed by an attempt to get individual legislators to voluntarily pledge to limit their future runs, but as you might imagine, holding legislators to their word without them being bound by law has proven very tricky. A constitutional amendment may be term limits' only remaining hope. It's worth a try—and the effort at least sends the message that when it comes to legislation, we do not believe "the more the better." Nor do we believe that people become more moral and wise the more time they spend simmering in the Swamp. Let's at least get some new blood in there, people with fresh ideas—and fewer long-standing ties to special interests in D.C. that make them forget who elected them.

The amendment process does not have to start in Congress, where you might well expect sentiment in favor of term limits to be weak. Constitutional amendments can begin in the same statehouses that must ultimately ratify them. However, if such an amendment needed a rhetorical boost, maybe the public could be persuaded to see term limits as part of a broader push for campaign reform. The whole concept of campaign reform hasn't always been popular with mainstream conservatives—who rightly fear it being used as an excuse to have the government subsidize incumbents' campaigns while limiting the ability of challengers to raise private-sector money. However, Trump's populist bent has made him more open to the idea.

Maybe Republicans could turn campaign reform into a conservative issue and in the process draw attention to one of the ugliest scandals in our political system, which is widespread voter fraud. Democrats like to pretend it doesn't happen—that it's just an excuse for Republicans to impose restrictions that will limit the ability of minorities to vote—but hidden-camera footage of Democratic officials talking about the long-standing practice of busing people in from other districts and sending illegals to the polls using other people's names suggests Republicans aren't just being paranoid.

In fact, one of the senators who has been the most vocal in criticizing Trump since the 2016 election, Minnesota's Al Franken, might never have been elected if we were serious about cracking down on voter fraud. According to Minnesota Majority, over a thousand felons ineligible to vote cast ballots in the election that put Franken in the Senate by just over three hundred votes. When the Democrats are so strongly opposed to measures such as voter ID cards and more careful screening for voting felons and voting illegals, you can bet they've crunched the numbers and figured out which party usually stands to gain from voter fraud. The Democrats aren't just in this game to increase democratic participation.

One thing Trump already seems to have gotten right is his desire to clamp down on the connection between lobbying and the White House.

One of the main reasons to consider reforms such as term limits, and one of the big reasons to favor transparency rather than secrecy in government, is that the longer politicians and government bureaucrats are in D.C., the cozier they become with the special interests who make themselves at home near the politicians' offices. Think how little time politicians spend back in their actual "home" districts compared to the time they spend in D.C. and its suburbs. Numerous trade organizations make their homes in or near

D.C., and they don't do it because that's where the conditions for factory production or open-air bazaars are best. They want to be there because that's where the people with the political clout to dole out subsidies and tweak regulations are.

No one is more effective in working those levers from the lobbyists' side than someone who has already been on the governmental side—not only because former legislators and their staffers know which regulations to evade, which forms to fill out, and which politician or staffer to butter up (or bribe), but also simply because veterans of government have connections. They don't just know whom to call, they already have the phone numbers, and their former colleagues are quite likely to listen to them—more likely, anyway, than to listen to one random citizen among 330 million calling up with a problem. Get in line, pal—unless of course we saw each other at the Gridiron correspondents' dinner last year or used to work in the same congressional office building. Then, hey, I might as well hear you out about this idea of yours about having the Commerce Department loan you money to send salesmen on a junket to China.

As noted earlier, Jack Abramoff sees the wisdom in Trump focusing not just on limiting lobbyists entering the administration but also, crucially, on limiting the ability of people to walk out of the administration and make a quick buck by transforming into well-connected lobbyists the moment they're out the door. Thus, Trump's five-year ban on administration officials lobbying when they leave.

President Obama, by contrast, claimed that central to his "hope and change" agenda would be a ban on lobbyists in his administration, and in practice, the ban was waived again and again, always with the (fairly reasonable) excuse that some of those former lobbyists really are experts on the industries they represented. Sure, you might just need them. Just don't let them go right back to lobbying.

It's not the existence of either political staffers or interest groups

alone that makes for a sleazy money trough for the well connected—
it's the government people and private-sector people transforming
back and forth into one another before your eyes. To mix meta-
phors for a moment, the Swamp has a constantly revolving door.

When they aren't technically transformed into lobbyists, landing
on corporate boards is a popular fate for many politicians who finally
extricate themselves from the purely governmental parts of the
Swamp, only to use their connections to the Swamp as their new
selling point. Often, they don't even leave D.C.; they just move offices (after a suitable pause to comply with lobbying regulations, or
with sufficient layers of legalistic protection) to a trade association or
corporate headquarters not far from the Capitol and continue milk-
ing the taxpayers. Like the former Harry Reid staffer who soon became a well-connected gambling commissioner, everyone somehow
exits Congress rich despite their ostensibly low salaries and desire to
be a humble "public servant."

Draining the Swamp does not just mean resisting the outside influence that special interests in the United States have over our government. We should put America first and reduce our involvement
in entangling foreign alliances.

I've already mentioned the ripples Trump set off among the elite
by suggesting that we should reduce U.S. involvement in the United
Nations. Why not take back our entire billion-dollar annual contribution? Just as problems like poverty are not solved simply by
throwing money at them, world peace is not guaranteed by the size
of the budget of that bureaucracy on the East River in New York.
We can still deal with nations in a friendly fashion—even make
treaties when necessary—without having to consult with a perma-
nent Security Council of one of the innumerable other subsidiary
parts of the UN apparatus.

Similarly, while our national defense should remain second to none, it is not clear that we make ourselves any safer by intervening in every military conflict around the globe, sometimes without even being sure about who all the sides doing the fighting are.

In March 2017, Republican senator Rand Paul of Kentucky angered his fellow Republican senator John McCain of Arizona by objecting to U.S. backing for the tiny Balkan country of Montenegro to enter NATO. NATO is not just a club of countries we like; NATO members are obliged to defend each other in the event of attack. We take on a responsibility and a risk with each and every member of that alliance. It's dangerous enough business—though perhaps necessary during the Cold War a generation ago—when the member countries are relatively peaceful ones such as the UK or France, which we do not expect to be invaded or embroiled in war anytime soon.

But Balkan nations such as Montenegro have been plagued by wars for centuries. As recently as the '90s, Montenegro partnered with Serbia and committed war crimes against neighboring Croatia. I want the people of those countries to be at peace and to be happy, but I do not want us to end up fighting all their battles. Remember, that's the tiny corner of the world that gave the rest of the planet World War I, and the general consensus now is that that war was both avoidable and largely pointless—but happened because complex entangling alliances sucked several nations into what should have been a local spat.

For his skepticism about NATO expansion, though, Paul was called an "agent of Putin" by an angry McCain. It's the sort of accusation President Trump has gotten used to himself if he shows the smallest sign of deviating from the militarist thinking of his party's McCain wing. War, like any other government project and maybe more so, is an expensive project that can easily go wrong. Let's not be too enthusiastic about entering into it or eager for a fight, even if we pride ourselves on winning when we do get into a fight.

Accusing Trump of being too cozy with the Russians has become an obsession for some on the left—people who just months earlier were criticizing Trump supporters as prone to conspiracy theories—but these critics on the left were oddly silent about Joe Biden and John Kerry both having relatives on the boards of Ukrainian fuel corporations around the time of the anti-Russian coup against that country's elected government.

Let's face it, Russia presses its case (westward) and the EU and United States press their case (eastward). Sometimes their interests will clash, and sometimes they'll need to talk things out. Trump's blunt but frank talk may be less likely to turn such tensions nuclear than the kind of Clintonian disingenuous, covert manipulations of foreign regimes and revolutions—in Europe, the Arab world, and Latin America—that characterized the Obama years and arguably the Bush years and many presidencies before that. If the Russians are dangerous, they're at their most dangerous when they're rendered paranoid by the West continually expanding NATO—which it promised not to do at the end of the Cold War—while pretending to have no designs beyond safeguarding democracy.

There's something oddly contradictory about Trump's critics talking about him as if he's a hothead liable to launch nukes for little or no reason and then condemning him for being too nice to Russia. The old Cold War establishment can be a bit like a bluffing high school bully, continually putting up a hostile front while pretending not to have done a thing, then feigning shock when it suddenly has a fight on its hands, the fight it craved all along—at which point, of course, the bully says the other guy started it.

Some of Trump's deal-making bravado might be a better formula for peace in Eastern Europe.

And after all, with over one hundred bases overseas and a U.S. military budget of about $600 billion, we ought to keep in mind that looming threat closer to home—the need to pay off that

$20 trillion federal debt. In the unlikely event that we have a little left over, there are American needs that probably ought to take priority over trying to transform every regime in the Middle East. (And Trump's call for a short-term increase in military spending is not necessarily at odds with the long-term goal of reducing spending: Stay out of wars, and in the long run, you avoid the most expensive part of having a military, after all.)

Far be it for me to suggest that we turn every inefficiently spent military dollar into an inefficiently spent domestic programs dollar, but a reduction in foreign commitments would make it easier to invest in infrastructure—crumbling roads and bridges in need of repair—right here at home. At the very least, paying down the debt means not having to spend over $200 billion a year just paying the interest on the federal debt. That's all money spent at the expense of all of us taxpayers, which wouldn't have to be spent if the D.C. elite were responsible enough to balance the books.

But spending is not the only indicator of the devastating impact that the federal government has on the economy. One that's harder to quantify but just as important is the mountain of regulation under which Americans struggle to operate. It may be the biggest obstacle to escaping the Swamp.

14. DRAINING BY DEREGULATING

Somebody has to tell the EPA that we don't need you monkeying around and fiddling around and getting in our business with every kind of regulation you can dream up. You're doing nothing more than killing jobs. It's a cemetery for jobs at the EPA.

—RICK PERRY

President Trump has shown a remarkable willingness to buck one of the biggest politically correct trends, effectively ending the days of treating global warming as an urgent crisis and an excuse for ever more regulation. He also declared an end to the "war on coal" that such regulations promoted. Good news for the economies of Kentucky, Pennsylvania, and West Virginia, but also good news for people relying on affordable energy today who are skeptical that a tiny, tiny possible rise in ocean levels a century from now is worth hamstringing our civilization today. Does anyone remember the hysteria several decades ago over the looming ice age? We would all freeze, we were warned. Hogwash.

One benefit of the left—media and activists alike—flying off the handle every time President Trump sends out a sharply worded message on Twitter is that it distracts them from the drier, more technical but extremely important things he's accomplishing, like rolling back regulations from the Obama years.

Obama was initially hailed as a president who understood the Constitution, because he'd been a constitutional law professor at the University of Chicago. That didn't stop him from complaining that Congress wasn't doing its job if it failed to support his policy ideas and threatening repeatedly to get the job done through executive orders if Congress wouldn't play along. Well, the whole reason the Constitution set up three branches of government was so that they wouldn't just play along and echo each other's will. When in doubt, the Founding Fathers preferred that our government do nothing. We're usually safest when it does. The scariest words someone can hear in their lifetime are: "We're with the government, and we are here to help you." If that ever happens to you, run the opposite way!

A frustrated President Obama turned to executive orders—or technically, more often to presidential memoranda—to issue new regulations on everything from overtime pay to family leave to border enforcement.

Trump vowed to roll back regulations when he took office, and one of the first concrete results was his directive to all the executive branch agencies to repeal two old regulations for each new one they create. Good idea.

The two-for-one rule of thumb sends a powerful message that the new default assumption is in favor of freedom, in favor of the Swamp doing less and the businesses regulated by it being permitted to do more.

No matter how well-intentioned regulations may be, they obviously, by definition, restrict businesses' options for producing goods and servicing their customers.

The National Association of Manufacturers, though by no means neutral on the issue, offers the disturbing estimate that regulation costs the U.S. economy as much as $2 trillion a year. The Heritage

Foundation estimates that regulations added during the Obama administration alone cost the economy $100 billion. The Mercatus Center at George Mason University puts the cost in more concrete, more frightening terms. They estimate that if regulation had simply been held constant at its 1980 levels—instead of executive branch agencies forever coming up with new ones—the U.S. economy would today be 25 percent larger than it is, meaning we've suffered a loss comparable to about $13,000 per capita.

Now think about all that people could buy, all they could create, all the opportunities they could offer other up-and-coming people if they had that much additional wealth at their disposal. Think of the ripple effects on the economies of struggling developing nations around the world.

Even if we assume, generously, that regulations achieve their stated aims, such as preventing workplace accidents or making food less likely to spoil, it is hard to believe they do so much good as to outweigh the good that could have been done with that lost $2 trillion. Extra wealth doesn't just go toward buying flashier lawn ornaments and bigger belt buckles. It also pays for health care, college tuitions, home heating, better food, new businesses, faster computers, safer cars, and every other imaginable improvement in human life, and then there are all the multiplier effects that occur when wealthier people have the luxury of taking new risks, trying out new ideas and new investments, traveling to meet and exchange ideas with people they wouldn't otherwise have encountered.

Destroy wealth and you impair humanity's chances to make things better. It's that simple.

You see, the creatures of the Swamp need to justify their existence. You can't have bureaucrats and expect them to sit idly by, believe it or not. They must justify their existence by mulling, creating, and enforcing new regulations. They dream of a world where everything is so regulated that absolutely nothing can go wrong. Unfortunately, to me that sounds more like an animal in a zoo cage than the liberty our Founding Fathers envisioned.

Frustrated owners and workers find themselves having to comply with regulations that they know make no sense. Movie theaters might have new design ideas that would make viewing more comfortable and easy, but good luck trying to redesign something as complex as a movie theater without running afoul of the very precise architectural formulas that building codes decree.

Jon Gabriel of the group FreedomWorks notes that the Code of Federal Regulations is now over 170,000 pages long, and it specifies not just, say, that factories shouldn't kill their neighbors with deadly fumes, but such petty things as proper pickle size, which you'd think pickle growers and pickle eaters could decide for themselves without the government imposing itself on the transaction. After all, the free market is a far better determiner of pickle size than the federal government.

Gabriel cites the "United States Standards for Grades of Pickles" as written by the Processed Products Branch of the Fruit and Vegetable Division of the Agricultural Marketing Service of the Department of Agriculture, and among other things they specify, in a long, lettered list: "(m) Misshapen pickles mean whole pickles that are crooked or otherwise deformed (such as nubbins). *Also see the definition for crooked pickles.* (n) Nubbin is a misshapen pickle that is not cylindrical in form, is short and stubby, or is not well developed."

The government also specifies that "reasonably good color in cured type means the typical skin color of the pickles ranges from light green to dark green and is reasonably free from bleached areas. Not more than 25 percent, by weight, of the pickles may vary markedly from such typical color. In mixed pickles, chow chow pickles, and pickle relish, all of the ingredients possess a reasonably uniform color typical for the respective ingredient. The pickles and other vegetable ingredients shall be free of off-colors."

Why are taxpayers—including, keep in mind, the non-pickle-eating taxpayers—subsidizing endless tiny business decisions that should be made in the free market? Sellers will penalize business partners who refuse to use clear terminology by refusing to work with them—or by suing them if they are deceitful enough. Customers will veer away from farmers and supermarkets who say *radish* when they mean *tomato*. Government doesn't have to be involved here—and that's true of most areas of the economy. How about Washington focus on bigger problems than judging the size of my vegetables?

It would be a big mistake—and the kind to which the left is prone—to think that "the imposition of costs on producers don't really matter because those costs just cut into the fat cats' profits."

As production costs rise, the prices businesses charge for their goods naturally rise as well—especially if all their competitors are raising prices at the same time, as is likely if they're all being subjected to roughly the same regulations. From the consumer's perspective (if the consumer knows a little basic economics), it doesn't matter how much profit businesses are making; what matters to the consumer is being worse off himself because it's harder to buy things. Regulations raise costs for virtually everyone, not just a few "greedy" manufacturers.

Furthermore, not only shouldn't one make the mistake of thinking that regulations will achieve the good ends, such as preventing auto crash deaths—since, for instance, accompanying fuel-economy standards might encourage smaller, lighter, more vulnerable cars—one shouldn't assume all regulations have good intentions behind them.

In fact, one of the most common purposes of regulation is to keep rich, powerful businesses rich and powerful at the expense of their newer, smaller upstart competitors. Have you ever noticed how every time some new regulatory initiative is being rolled out, whether it's tighter limits on smokestack emissions or the banning of certain food additives, there are always at least some big businesses that are surprisingly eager to play along and announce that they, too, support the regulations? The activists or regulators who pushed for the new rules are delighted to be able to point to these allies as evidence that "even business agrees with us," and the businesses are happy to bask in the glow of good PR, as they appear to be the "good corporate citizens" of the week.

But it's almost always nonsense straight from the heart of the Swamp.

The businesses that are playing along usually do so (we can safely guess) not only because they like the publicity but, more creepily, often because they know that the new regulations will make life harder for their competitors than for their own businesses. Think about it. If there's a new safety regulation being considered that would make it illegal to sell a car without a built-in emergency alert signal—and you happened to just start production on a car model that has such a signal, but your main competitor didn't—isn't there a heightened likelihood that you will suddenly "realize" that all good cars should have emergency signals built in?

You might even sincerely believe that you have no ulterior motive in trying to outlaw those other, more reckless and irresponsible car manufacturers. You're just thinking about the needs of the public! You're a humanitarian! You may even deserve an award or something. Or at least several more million dollars than you would have made otherwise.

The result of all these layers of regulation isn't just an abstract "unfairness," either. They contribute to the stagnation of our economy.

Given the amazing advances in technology that have occurred in the past three decades, we could easily be growing at a rate of 5 percent per year if we weren't held back by rules that insist we keep doing things the same old way. In a completely regulated economy, every experiment becomes something that may require a special waiver or permit or new license. Rich people may, if they're feeling lucky, dispatch their lawyers to deal with all of it. Middle-class and poor people may not even dare to try.

To some on the left, the resulting stagnation doesn't even matter. Some think economic growth is actually a bad thing. It might lead to greater income inequality or more pollution or gentrification of old neighborhoods. Historically, these problems work themselves out better when left to the private sector, but it doesn't matter—the most cautious people on the left would rather not risk it.

One side effect is U.S. companies fleeing overseas—and another is foreign companies being less likely to invest here—because there are plenty of corners of the world where U.S.-style regulations aren't in place to interfere with production. Granted, there may be extreme cases in which we might all agree those other nations ought to have some regulation, or at least basic laws against fraud and assault, in place. I'm not condoning every abusive act committed by a Chinese sweatshop owner.

But instead of complaining that "capitalism" is shipping jobs overseas, let's consider the possibility that regulations are doing so, and then let's see if we can roll them back. Let's also cut the United States' unusually high corporate tax rate while we're at it. That's a combination that should bring back jobs.

Failure to do so is one of the big reasons that Trump saw a surge of support in the 2016 election from union members and Midwest blue-collar workers the likes of which the Republican Party hadn't seen since Reagan. People are indeed hurting out there, and their pain is exacerbated, not alleviated, by most of the state's interventions.

If you don't like having a disgruntled population of "deplorables" on your hands, make life easier for the companies that employ them.

Let the United States be a place where businesses can operate without fear of interference and there'll be less need to scratch our heads and wonder why American cars are being built in Thailand or American cell phones in China.

Another perverse side effect of having so many regulations is that instead of spurring companies to adopt the best, newest methods of doing things, the regulations are almost always based on the old habits of the largest, laziest, most established companies. Even Franklin Roosevelt's New Deal turned to leaders in industry to set the rules for his planning boards and commissions. They weren't about to regulate themselves out of business, but if they regulated some little guys out of business, well, tough luck.

Mercifully, the government has kept its hands off the computer industry, for the most part, but if it now intervened in a big way, do you think it would mandate the most cutting-edge practices gleaned from some unknown young night-owl genius geek coding the next big leap in quantum computing in his parents' basement? Do you think the government would have understood what was going on in Steve Jobs's parents' garage back in the 1970s?

Hell no. The government, run by elderly men, most of whom have never run a real business, would probably turn to someone they might be familiar with. The government has no role picking winners and losers; the free market will dictate that decision every time.

You might say heartlessly that the start-ups should just fulfill all the regulatory rules and then work even harder to top what the old guys are doing. But what if what the old guys are doing—now codified as industry standards that everyone must follow—is precisely what the newcomers think is holding everyone back? What if their leap ahead would be made possible by ignoring the big guys' way of doing things?

And to put it less glamorously, what if it's just cheaper for the newcomers to do it a new way that doesn't quite comply with the old industry standard but gets the job done? Sometimes, finding a way that's a little less expensive is the key to getting a new company off the ground, and without that first step, it would never be around to come up with even bigger and better ways of doing things later that lead to greater safety, greater efficiency, and unforeseen changes that leave the old ways and the old rulebook in the dust.

Get the red tape out of the way and let people try something different.

More terrifying than government's impulse to regulate, though, are the truly delusional moments when it decides it knows how to innovate better than millions of private entrepreneurs do. The people operating in the private sector are fighting for their financial lives and risking their own wealth while hunting around rapidly for new, better ideas that will give them an edge on the competition.

And yet along comes a community organizer from Chicago like Barack Obama, who seems to view business with contempt, to announce with great fanfare that government, in its wisdom, is going to create "innovation hubs" across America, mini-cities where new business and technology ideas will take off. How about you? Has your life been transformed by all the government's innovation hubs recently?

Innovation happens wherever and whenever entrepreneurs and inventors in the market think it can most profitably happen—usually not under the thumb of government—and the suggestion that government has a better track record in predicting which industries to subsidize, which entrepreneurs to reward, and which inventions to invest in is simply laughable.

The U.S. federal government announcing that now there will be innovation is like a king of old decreeing that this year there shall be a bountiful harvest of crops. The best thing the king can do is leave the farmers alone, and the best thing the federal government can do is keep its taxes and regulations out of the way. President Trump seems to understand that.

At least Trump has worked extensively in the private sector and knows how many regulatory hurdles you have to jump through to get things done—especially in real estate in New York City. His book *Trump: The Art of the Deal* is largely an account of how to time all the interlocking regulatory permissions you need just right so that construction on a project can actually begin. Construction teams won't start work until you've got investors on board, investors won't come on board until they're assured you've got all the necessary permits, and yet the permits often aren't forthcoming unless they know there's a big enough financial investment in the project to warrant speeding up the glacial permitting process. It's almost logically impossible to make it all happen, and it takes a rare combination of charm and pushiness to do it—but it should be easy.

The goal is to build things and make things, not see who can navigate the obstacle course we've created. Like many property owners, Trump has found himself navigating regulatory obstacles even when doing something as simple as putting up an American flag at his Mar-a-Lago estate in Florida in 1985. His flag, in classic Trump fashion, was about three times as big and twice as high as spottily enforced Palm Beach regulations technically allowed, the rule being four feet by six feet for the flag and forty-two feet for the pole. The town council fined him hundreds of dollars a day for the violation, and after a six-month legal battle, the fines were waived in return for his agreeing to donate $100,000 to veterans charities and lower the offending flagpole from about eighty feet to seventy feet.

Multiply Trump's annoyance over that little battle times the hundreds of such fights he's had over real estate development in New York City and other localities and you get some idea how skeptical the man probably is about regulation.

Contrast Trump's experience with that of Obama or Hillary Clinton. Both of them have come to be skeptical of markets and trusting of government regulation largely because they've never had normal jobs that forced them to jump through those regulatory hurdles. The closest they came to honest jobs before becoming political officeholders was being lawyers, law professors, and legal counsel to political foundations. They never really had to worry about payrolls, delivery schedules, equipment upgrades, or winning back dissatisfied customers.

Hillary went directly from being a law student to being a congressional legal aide and lawyer to the big, politically connected foundation the Children's Defense Fund, then to a similar foundation in Arkansas and a job at the Rose Law Firm. Soon, though, her main claim to fame would be being the Arkansas governor's wife. Since then, she hasn't looked back. Her contribution to the current sharing/gig economy has mainly been to threaten Uber with more regulation in one campaign speech in 2016, as if the problem with today's start-ups is that they don't look like large, old, unionized industries.

Obama first worked as a community organizer—basically someone who teaches many other people how to work the political system to get subsidies and special-interest political attention—in the years in between his undergraduate and law school education, and he returned to that role after Harvard Law, moving between the worlds of organizing, political foundation management, voter-registration drives, and teaching at University of Chicago Law School for a few years before being elected to the Illinois state senate in 1996 at age thirty-five and the U.S. Senate eight years later.

Obama told a crowd in Virginia during his 2012 reelection campaign, "Somebody helped to create this unbelievable American system that we have that allowed you to thrive. Somebody invested in roads and bridges. If you've got a business—you didn't build that. Somebody else made that happen. The internet didn't get invented on its own. Government research created the internet so that all the companies could make money off the internet." He wasn't so much describing a carefully thought-out theory of economics as revealing his implicit picture of how politics works.

In Obama's world, you get things done by organizing political pressure. That's simply the universe he's lived in. It's not one of costs and benefits, it's one of vocal political winners and silent political losers. Business decisions are an afterthought. The heavy lifting, he imagines, is done by the people who decided at foundation meetings whether to make appeals to the mayor, or in D.C. committee meetings whether to allocate more funds to something. Mere businessmen are tiny end users of the system the political people, the important people, shape.

The idea of government being a terrible nuisance to productive citizens is alien to him.

If regulation were such a good idea, one might at least hope that it yielded more benefits than costs—more lives saved than destroyed, more pollution eliminated than wasteful new procedures created. Interestingly, though, the proponents of regulation, usually but not always Democrats, have always fought tooth and nail against making basic cost-benefit analysis an automatic part of each new regulation.

There is now a special office for making such assessments, and under Trump each cabinet-level agency has been asked to create a committee for reviewing existing regulations to see which ones have the biggest net negative impact on the sectors of the economy affected by them.

You might ask, "But what about safety?" If we leave things up to the marketplace, won't companies completely ignore safety in favor of making a quick buck? Well, once in a while, yes, under any system of rules, market based or governmental, there will be bad decisions, but consider all the incentives the market creates to avoid disasters.

To put it bluntly, your customers aren't going to be around too long to give you repeat business if you harm them . . . or, worse, if you kill them. Dead customers also aren't going to recommend you to their friends. Furthermore, customers can shop around, and they really can sort out for themselves, or with help from private-sector customer reviews, how much safety (or anything else) they think is worth paying for. Dad might want speed, but Mom may refuse to pay for something without air bags and shatterproof glass.

And it's not just up to the individual customer's judgment even in a completely free market. Manufacturers can get sued if they make something in a misleadingly dangerous way, and they know it—and if they forget, their insurance companies know it and will hike their premiums accordingly. Your amusement park is going to pay a lot more for insurance if customers keep flying off the roller coaster, believe me.

I suppose to some that may sound like a crass way of putting it, but then, the basic laws of economics sound harsh to some people. They aren't really. What's cruel is ignoring them and thinking that a few rules written by a big-government bureaucracy can suspend the laws of physics or change the laws of economics.

If economics sounds harsh, you should be more scared by the fact that a lot of the dry regulations on the books are there only because some politician gave a speech that sounded not at all harsh. It sounded warm and fuzzy and positive, like "innovation hubs"—and then the boring bureaucrats, with some help from their well-connected industry friends, had to figure out some way to make all that fuzzy poetry into a bunch of rules with truly harsh penalties attached to them, and harsh consequences for the economy.

Chop away at it all, set the American economy free, and let this nation soar again in ways we cannot predict.

And if you want some inspiring suggestions that don't fly in the face of the laws of economics, read on for my suggestions for an agenda that will truly unlock American greatness.

15. DARE TO DRAIN

Being willing to donate the taxpayers' money is not the same as being willing to put your own money where your mouth is.

—THOMAS SOWELL

Don't feel sorry for Washington, D.C.

Every mistake the federal government makes, every embarrassment it suffers, every scandal it endures is a disaster paid for with other people's money. It is never their own money on the line; *you* always pick up the tab. Every harebrained scheme they come up with is one they feel comfortable risking in part because they will not be the ones who bear the consequences in the end. The ecosystem of the Swamp is fundamentally parasitic, and the nation's citizens are the host.

If the current mood in politics is more "populist" than traditionally conservative, liberal, or libertarian, it's partly because the public has lost patience waiting for the policy experts of all stripes to fix things. Populism is a loosely defined political mood, and for over a century, it has included figures as diverse as William Jennings Bryan (who disliked gold-backed currency because he thought it would be bad for debt-racked farmers), Ross Perot (whose suspicions of trade agreements like NAFTA are echoed in Trump's policies), and Pat Buchanan (who emphasized the idea of national sovereignty at a time when most of the Republican Party was riding high on the United States' default victory in the Cold War and dreaming of a "New World Order").

What they had in common was the suspicion that whatever those "leaders" and "experts" in D.C. were up to, it was more self-serving than publicly beneficial. They could smell the rot coming from the Swamp even if they didn't pretend to be able to sort out exactly which forms of vegetation and animal life were causing it. And guess what? It is in politicians' best interest for survival in the Swamp that they don't work too hard in shining a light on the creatures dwelling there.

The same goes for a big swath of the American public today. One of the reasons they don't get as outraged as the press at every instance of Trump glossing over details or dismissing critics with a joke is that they know the people carrying all the detailed charts and graphs probably aren't really on their side anyway. The "experts" are often just there to put a pretty front on the Swamp, rendering us passive to its growth and putrefaction. Enough of that.

To President Trump, in addition to my unsolicited advice from the two preceding chapters (deregulate and limit terms, reduce lobbying, and establish a more businesslike approach to running the government), I would say, keep listening to the general public and not the noise in Washington. The best aspect of populism is its orientation against parasitic elites and in favor of the overwhelming majority of the population, even as specific policies come and go.

One of the reasons so many of Trump's fellow billionaires were panicked when his political fortunes began rising during the 2016 primary season was that they know he doesn't really need to prove himself to the elite anymore. He's already got billions of his own.

He's traveled. He's done TV, golfed with celebrities, dated and married glamorous and successful women, and been a doting father to successful children who adore him. Those worried billionaires having conferences about how to stop the Trump Train were worried that he'd now turn his attention to proving himself to the masses kind enough to entrust him with votes. The elite aren't worried Trump will destroy the economy, undermine free markets, cause a collapse of global trade.

Their real fear is that he just might be the guy who knocks over the trough, ending subsidies and special favors for the elite. I hope he really will be that guy.

Obviously, I don't hate the rich. I wouldn't be saying nice things about Trump if I did. However, there are the rich who got there the old-fashioned way—coming up with new ideas and selling them to a willing public (or just being very efficient at selling the old ideas—nothing wrong with that). And then there are the rich, usually not working directly for the government but very chummy with it, who got there by using regulations and subsidies to tilt the playing field ever so slightly in their own favor.

Remember all those trade associations and lobbyists who are headquartered in D.C.? They aren't there to look out for you. That's what creates room for a populist political figure such as Trump to take on the role of tribune of the people. An awful lot of people seem to have decided at the last minute to trust him, people who didn't tell pollsters they were planning to vote for him. They sensed that even if they couldn't fully predict which policies he'd pursue, he wasn't just going to sell them the usual op-eds and think tank papers that sound public spirited and end up helping only a few well-connected movers and shakers. Candidate Trump was spot on when, at various rallies, he would loudly pronounce, "What the hell do you have to lose?" Middle America tried the experts, they tired of the revolving-door politicians, and so they took a chance on a self-made businessman.

He sounds like he hates the Swamp, in fact. That's *the point*!

Now, I simply say to the president: Keep your pledge to drain the Swamp.

Throughout the history of the Swamp's growth, for every politician caught up in some scandal, there has been a politician who promised reform. They all do, to some extent, whether it's the pledge to create a "kinder, gentler" America from George H. W. Bush, the "New Covenant" of Bill Clinton, or the "hope and change" of Barack Obama. Even the most well-meaning politicians, though, will find that there are powerful incentives to settle back into business as usual once they arrive in the Swamp.

Once you're in Washington, no matter how many emails you get from constituents, the voices of the public will never be quite as loud as the voices of the lobbyists and fellow politicians sitting right there in the room with you, day in and day out—including the ones pleading for more spending and more special favors at endless committee hearings. Hardly anyone marches up Capitol Hill to say, "Thanks, but we don't really need that spending program that's targeted at us anymore. All set."

Once you're in Washington, you also won't hear too many of the Swamp creatures saying, "We might lose that one tight congressional district in the next election cycle if we tell the truth about how badly that program needs to end, but principle is more important than electoral victory, so let's go ahead and cut the program." You don't hear too many Swamp creatures saying, "Cutting these programs will make our campaign fund-raising harder and be unpopular in the short term, but it's the right thing to do, so let's forge ahead."

You will instead hear an endless chorus saying, "These programs will help people in need who may weep very publicly on television if you end their programs—and some very rich people who may not weep but will stop doling out campaign contributions and inviting us on fun junkets to visit the exotic islands where they're holding their conferences this year—so maybe next year we can try trimming that item a bit, budget negotiations permitting, but right now just isn't strategically wise. Soon, though, maybe."

And it never ends, and the Swamp never gets drained. Unless something very unusual—something strange and random, really—happens. Maybe Trump can be that strange thing. He doesn't need anyone's money. He doesn't have to bow and scrape for approval. He even seems to enjoy offending people sometimes. Good. Maybe he can become that person who cuts a path through the Swamp and does the right thing. He should avoid the voices counseling moderation and compromise, because what they're usually saying, in veiled language, is, "The Swamp works. The Swamp makes sense once you really get to know it, once you learn to love its ways. Don't drain it. Don't even rock the boat."

Don't listen to those business-as-usual voices. To borrow a favorite word from the crazy anti-Trump protestors: resist.

The haters are going to hate—and scream—whether you make a 1 percent cut in a single program's budget or a 90 percent cut in every program's budget, so you might as well aim for the latter while you're at it. Better yet, cut nearly all programs' budgets to zero. You'll have more money to spend on a few essential things like military defense and fulfilling commitments to impoverished elderly people.

They say Ronald Reagan didn't pay any attention to public opinion polls. Given how unscientific polls really are—as we were all reminded when Trump won the election despite those "2 percent chance of winning" claims—Reagan probably had the right idea. The poll that matters is the one that takes place on Election Day.

And frankly, Trump doesn't strike me as a guy who's going to spend his first four years in office sweating and worrying about whether he'll be reelected the next time. He might as well forge ahead and fulfill as much of his agenda as he can.

Let the Swamp creatures howl.

Really fulfilling the Trump mandate for reform, though, will mean keeping the pressure on Washington at all times.

One of the establishment's main weapons will be trying to deflect attention onto Trump himself. Everything he does that even appears the slightest bit eccentric or outside the bounds of normal procedure will be touted as evidence that the republic is falling apart, that the Russians are taking over, that the fascists are taking over, that the big corporations are taking over, or whatever paranoid idea is the weekly bee in the bonnet of his leftist opponents.

But love him or hate him, Trump should not be the one on trial here. What about the rest of Washington? Does Trump loom so large in the minds of the left that they think he'll block out our view of the Swamp altogether? Sorry, we're not falling for it anymore. Americans didn't send Trump to Washington to clean up Trump. They sent Trump to Washington to clean up Washington. Let's stay focused on the mission.

That means now is a better time than ever for those few journalists who are sincerely concerned about making the country a greater place to look beyond Trump to all the routine corruption and crazy spending of the sort surveyed in this book. We Americans differ on philosophy, religion, and more, but we have a shared interest in draining this Swamp. We all benefit when its leeches and strangling vines are beaten back.

The best way to achieve this is to hold people accountable for their wrongdoing for a change. Many Clinton supporters went into the 2016 election so dead set against Trump being president that they were willing to overlook decades of wrongdoing by the Clintons. A Trump staffer speaks briefly to a Russian and it's supposed to foretell the death of the republic, but the Clintons take billions from Saudi Arabia even while shaping U.S. policy, and it's just yawn-inducing business as usual, no big deal, go back to sleep, drown peacefully in the Swamp without any protest.

Hell no.

If you want to make the most of Trump's time in office, push him even further in the direction to which he's naturally inclined: rewarding productive behavior and punishing failure. If you think there's corruption and waste throughout Washington, by all means call upon him to fire people.

Liberals are a pessimistic bunch, and I think they naturally sympathize with anyone who might be fired, laid off, or turned out of office—but that's how you get people out of the spots where they're not very useful and not only liberate resources to be used by someone better suited for the spot but liberate the fired person as well to go find some better fit elsewhere, some more effective way to be a productive member of society.

Remember, government is supposed to exist for the American people as a whole. It's not supposed to be a jobs program—and certainly not a giant slush fund—just for the people lucky enough to be on the inside and employed by the government itself. With government at all levels consuming about 40 percent of the national income per year, that would be one awfully big, expensive welfare program. "Welfare" in the narrow sense of poverty relief for the few poorest Americans is pretty cheap by comparison and a small slice of the mammoth Washingtonian pie—though poverty relief, too, can be done better by volunteerism and the private sector, especially when companies are liberated to expand and hire new people.

So I'd love it if Trump said, "You're fired!" to whole cabinet agencies.

Department of Commerce, you think we need you to tell businesses what to do when they should be making decisions and hawking their wares on their own? Get out of the way!

Department of Agriculture, you think we need you to prop up big farms instead of just letting them compete like any other businesses, the big ag businesses taking their chances on the marketplace alongside family farms? You're fired!

Department of Housing and Urban Development, you think your squalid housing projects have improved family cohesion despite decades of mismanagement and crime? You're fired!

Department of Energy bureaucrats giving subsidies to well-connected, overhyped hippie projects that have virtually no chance of becoming price competitive with oil or other forms of energy already at hand? Get out!

Just keep hacking away at the Swamp vegetation—and do it fast. In the extremely unlikely event something gets cut that turns out later to have been useful, I have not the slightest doubt that Congress will happily vote to appropriate the money needed to bring it back into existence later. Expanding government is always far easier than shrinking it. So err on the side of getting rid of everything that we can live without, now.

There'll be howls of protest, of course, both within and beyond the Swamp itself. There will be campus vigils and angry newspaper editorials. There might be a sit-in by congressional Democrats. That's all the more reason to hope the current president is different from the mushy ones who preceded him. Trump should remain the man the public elected—the man his "base" elected.

For generations, the liberal press has played the subtle, hypnotic game of applauding politicians for "growing in office," which has always meant becoming more like everyone else in office, which is to say, more liberal than they were when they first got to town and dared contemplate making some cuts or reforms. They'll try the same thing with Trump, attempting to lure him with the carrot of calling him reasonable and moderate when he affirms conventional D.C. wisdom, once they get exhausted trying to use the stick of calling him a dangerous extremist.

Make no mistake about it, even if the press throws in the occasional nod to the concerns that got Trump elected—saying they concede there are some programs that are wasteful or trade deals that could have been negotiated with slightly greater transparency— the press's destination is always the same: right back to the heart of the Swamp and business as usual. The press has cozy relationships with establishment politicians and big-government agencies just like big businesses and organized pressure groups do. The longer people have been in D.C., the more relationships they have with other Swamp dwellers and the more protective they're likely to be of those relationships. To avoid sounding out of touch with their viewers or constituents back home, they can tout their relationships with those in power as evidence they're "in the know" and "getting things done."

The very ties that ought to make the public suspicious—and are beginning to have that very effect—are the ones the Swamp dwellers have spent decades cultivating. The incestuous ties were there from the beginning but took leaps forward each time there was a big expansion in the Swamp: in the Progressive Era under Teddy Roosevelt and war-propaganda-orchestrating Woodrow Wilson, in the Depression Era under Franklin Roosevelt's New Deal, and during and after Lyndon Johnson's Great Society.

Each time, the Swamp's vines became more entangled around

business—the early twentieth-century trusts, the Blue Eagle business partners of the mid-twentieth, and the subsidy-dependent pub-
lic/private partnerships of the late twentieth century—and more
entangled around media, too. Woodrow Wilson and his World War
I military practically created the Madison Avenue publicity firms.
Big newspapers like *The New York Times* would become ardent defenders of the New Deal programs. The major TV networks, back
when there were only about three, showed the world the heartstring-
tugging pictures that made all the Great Society programs seem
like the only answer to poverty and racism.

All those tools and more will be arrayed now against any attempt
to change course, the users of those tools more openly willing than
ever to vilify opponents, denigrate their relatives, turn reasonable
policy suggestions into fodder for late-night sketch comedy, and in
general shape the narratives that people inattentively assume to be
reality.

Not that there aren't a few of us out here making other noises
these days—reminding people that markets still have answers when
government seems to have run out of them, reminding people that
individual initiative can still do more to change the world than all
the media's sob stories and ever-changing reasons for outrage.

The best way for President Trump to counter the clatter of big-
government voices in mainstream media—and in a big chunk of
new media, thanks to sites like Salon that lean far to the left—is to
keep on tweeting!

I know, I know, you've heard many anti-Trump critics clucking
their tongues and saying that his use of the internet message service
Twitter is the clearest evidence that Trump's too angry and isn't
"presidential" enough. But how can the same experts who spent the
past two decades calling for "transparency" in government be un-

happy that the president is tweeting and letting us know very, very directly what's on his mind? If anything, we should probably worry about presidents holding back instead of tweeting, or leaving all tweeting to boring staff members. I say, tweet away, Mr. President! Don't hold back!

There have been rumors Twitter might suspend the president's account, which I think would be a big mistake—bad for Trump, bad for Twitter, bad for democracy, and even bad for mainstream media. Bad for America.

Trump would no longer be able to do an end run around the bias of the mainstream media. At last count, Trump social media accounts are followed by over one hundred million people. One hundred million! That's more than the entirety of the liberal left "mainstream media's" audience combined! They would be able to take tiny snippets of what he said, out of context, the way they have with other politicians for decades, and piece those snippets together into whatever narrative they wanted the American people to absorb. And with the press becoming more and more openly hostile to Trump and unapologetically part of the left-wing "resistance," it would be very easy for them to stick to the same narrow leftist narrative about what's going on. If they say all that matters is whether Trump says something about Russia, or about Islam, that's what you'll hear. They know not everyone will catch each press conference and see each correction that puts things in a clearer light.

With Twitter, for all its flaws and bizarre little feuds, you get Trump—or anyone else—unfiltered. Even if that means that media veterans like me have to share the stage with millions of other voices, I say it's a very healthy development, and I don't mind a bit. It must be a little like watching the era of the printing press begin and thousands of new voices suddenly get added to the tiny handful of princes and lords who had previously called all the shots. I'd rather have the president be part of that dialogue than have the mainstream media go back to their favorite game: pretending you can only hear from the important people by watching and listening to mainstream media.

Let it all hang out.

The furor over guerilla news sources such as Matt Drudge and Mike Cernovich shows the power alternative voices have. Outside the usual channels, stories sometimes come to you.

Such was the case when Hannah Giles approached my former producer Sergio Gor and his friend Tom Qualtere at a Washington restaurant in 2009. Giles, Andrew Breitbart, and others wanted to prove ACORN (the Association of Community Organizations for Reform Now) was willing to engage in illegal activities to further its get-out-the-vote and bring-in-the-government-subsidies mission.

Giles dressed up as if she were a prostitute and was seen on hidden camera footage getting advice from an ACORN staffer about concealing illegal professions from authorities while getting aid. The resulting bad publicity saw ACORN deprived of funds by Congress within months and shut down within a year (though elements of the organization live on under other names).

If something truly shocking happens in the Trump White House and none of the usual bland reporters or straightlaced government spokesmen quite want to talk about it, I for one would love to have a highly communicative president spouting off about what's going on. Tweet on!

In this ongoing battle, it will also be important to remember that the Swamp is not just something created by the left. Fight the whole "establishment" because it's just as dangerous as the liberal opposition.

One of the reasons the world is suddenly looking at populist figures such as Trump with new respect is that both liberalism and conservatism have blown it so badly over the past several decades.

Liberalism was originally supposed to be a political philosophy that protected the individual, but over the course of the twentieth century, it transformed into a philosophy of protecting government against critics, especially against pro-capitalist critics. The Democratic Party became the masters of talking about the little guy while using the little guy as an excuse to make bigger and bigger government—big and *distant* and quite beyond the control of the average little guy. But not to worry! Liberal politicians would at least pretend that they could watch out for your interests without much input from you, and if they need a growing portion of your wallet and more and more regulatory encroachments on your lifestyle to do it, well, so be it. You probably didn't know how to live your own life intelligently anyway. Leave it to the experts.

It would be comforting to believe that because conservatism, in the form of the Republican Party, opposed this transformation within liberalism, all it takes to defend freedom is electing Republicans. The sad truth, though, is once politicians and those who work with them become parts of the Swamp, political party—even political philosophy—doesn't count. Most of the money in Washington isn't flowing to fringe left-wing organizations. It's flowing to big-ticket items like Medicare and Social Security that both parties are afraid to alter, and to countless government contractors, often old pals of members of Congress (coincidentally, of course), who get paid to do virtually nothing and to do it slowly, but as part of some umbrella function that sounds too boring to attract attention or controversy, such as accounting, surveying, land management, statistics compiling, and so on.

The establishment Republicans can be even more dangerous than the liberal Democrats at times, because Republicans know how to coat every wasteful program in a thin veneer that sounds market friendly, so that even fiscally conservative voters think they're getting something for their buck. If you want to waste money and you have a conservative as opposed to liberal Congress member in your district (where your vote and perhaps your employees' votes are needed by the Congress member), just frame your request as a "Homeland Security" energy project or maybe a "faith-based nonprofit" effort instead of calling it a "green economy initiative" or a "multiculturalism center."

You get to waste the taxpayers' money and hire your friends regardless. And most members of Congress don't want that process stopped whether they have a *D* or an *R* after their names. All that matters—matters far more than party loyalty and far more than stated political ideology—is keeping those constituents back in the district (and anyone else who might help out with a campaign contribution) happy.

When in doubt, trust members from both parties to suck up to people with a lot of money who sound like they're from professions too neutral and too essential to belong to just the right or left, like banking. Sometimes the right likened Obama to a Communist, but it never stopped him from hiring people from Goldman Sachs.

So, while TV pundits like me—and activists in the street—fight over right versus left proposals, the Swamp mostly keeps gurgling away, doling out money to its rich friends that won't nudge the country right or left, just ensure that a bigger and bigger portion of its wealth sinks into the Swamp and linked waterways.

It's amazing, really, that with so much of the business of the Swamp being about taking money and redistributing it to the last people who'd ever need it, the Swamp creatures—of both the left and the right—still manage to give such idealistic speeches and sound, at least around election time, so preoccupied by the national well-being.

But as we've seen in this book, catch even the tiniest glimpse behind the mask and you'll usually find that the Swamp dwellers are some pretty sick customers. For instance, Democrat Representative Beto O'Rourke from Texas plans to try winning away the Senate seat of Republican Ted Cruz in 2018, and he talks a good game—an almost Trumpian game—about being a man of the people who hopes that ditching PACs, polls, and political consultants will give his campaign vigor of the sort that will make him the first Democrat elected to the Senate from Texas in decades. However, it's worth noting that in the 1990s O'Rourke had been arrested for both burglary and drunk driving. Is this really what a reformist looks like by congressional standards? I guess so.

I'll say this for Texans, though. They understand better than perhaps citizens of any other state in the union one important potential solution to the problem of the Swamp. We should place a bigger emphasis on states' rights against federal government power.

If people—including Beto O'Rourke or any of us—have a hard time managing our own lives, of which we have such up-close and personal knowledge, how much worse must we inevitably be at managing the lives of other people far away? That principle holds for central economic planning boards trying to run industries they don't understand (whether in the United States or the old USSR), and it holds for a single city on the Eastern Seaboard trying to tell everyone from Texas to North Dakota how to live and what to do with 40 percent of their income.

Local authority knows best, and the more we can devolve political decision-making to states and localities, the better.

Now the first objection that tends to come up when this idea is raised in an American context is usually inspired by memories of the mistreatment of blacks prior to the Civil War and in the subsequent Jim Crow years, as if every state longs for freedom just so it can turn around and oppress people. Even if that were likely in the twenty-first century, the federal government could always reserve the power, outlined in the Constitution under the post–Civil War amendments, to intervene in cases of basic civil liberties violations. More relevant in the modern context, though, is whether states should be allowed to experiment with managing their own health care and welfare-spending affairs.

It's not only that they have a better handle on local needs than the feds. It's also that all of us stand to benefit from the knowledge gained from fifty new laboratories of policy experimentation. Maybe we really can't agree on one best way to do things—maybe I'll argue for laissez-faire and always be greeted by people who think big government sounds like a great new idea that we haven't yet given a fair shake. But at least with fifty states given some leeway to try things, we might be better able to see what works, and even if we still come to no consensus, Americans will have more freedom to "vote with their feet" and go to the places that best suit their needs.

Right now, we have fifty states in name, but the growth of the federal government over the past century means that states end up having to behave in very homogeneous ways, especially if they want to get federal money for things like Medicaid and road repair, to which the feds typically attach conditions. Our way *and* the highway, you might say.

Competition between states for business and for new taxpaying citizens, like competition between suppliers in the marketplace, also has the great advantage of enabling reality to render a verdict on bad ideas even without any explicit debate taking place on the policy in question. Sometimes we don't really know why, say, one method of teaching leads to improved grades and another causes them to plummet even if very earnest education experts have debated the subject for years. We may only know that parents trapped in an area doing things the bad way decide to flee and that parents who hear about good schools in another area decide to move there.

We can't all be philosophers, and when the experts think they know the reasons for differential results, they could be wrong—much like smart CEOs who make bad predictions about which new products will sell. The important thing is that we still have the freedom to switch when things go wrong. The left's answer is usually to keep everyone trapped in the failing system or state and insist that if we all "come together as one" instead of jumping ship, surely next time everything will turn out better. That's dangerous. That's unfair. It doesn't have to be that way.

Let New York be New York, if it insists, and let Texas be Texas. Some leftists are coming around to this point of view, ironically, since they're suddenly so eager to see left-leaning states like California veer off and escape "Trump's America." Let them! And if Texas decides it wants to go even further than Trump in a government-shrinking, reformist direction, let them veer off, too. Texas has a big independent streak and was actually a separate, independent republic for a short time in the nineteenth century. Without having to go that far, we could still give states a much longer tether than the federal government has given them in recent decades.

There's also talk within California every few years of breaking that big state up into three smaller states. Sure. If local is better, many such experiments are possible. Letting people go their own way needn't be a catastrophe.

This impulse to give local people control over their own affairs may also be one of the best ways to understand some of the nationalist parts of Trump's agenda that the left finds the most off-putting. As with Brexit—the UK's peaceful departure from the European

Union—the United States can reaffirm its national sovereignty without becoming an enemy toward other nations.

In theory, we already have national borders, including one to the south between the United States and Mexico. You wouldn't know it from the way we let people wander across it, then just catch them and drop them back on the Mexican side until they try to sneak in again later. Is the United States even a country if it does nothing to defend its borders?

Democratic presidents and members of Congress seem to have understood, until Trump turned it into an issue they thought they could use against him, that some amount of credible enforcement is necessary if borders are to have any meaning. Hillary Clinton and Obama supported extensive fence construction along the U.S.-Mexican border. Clinton admitted as much in one of her 2016 debates against Trump. It seems to be a point of pride when she does it but evidence of xenophobia and hate when Trump pushes the same idea, at least to the thinking of pro-Clinton media.

Trump's Mexican border wall would make workable and practical an already-existing policy that has previously been treated as a joke by Mexican and U.S. authorities alike. Few people declared the moderate-sounding Mitt Romney a xenophobic anti-Mexican hater when he proposed a stronger border fence aimed at shoring up the same policy, basic border security, during his 2012 presidential campaign. Is everything scarier when Trump says it? Maybe because people think he might actually keep his word instead of making empty gestures? (Of course, it would have been hard to declare Romney a complete anti-Mexican bigot when his own father was born in Mexico, but that's a technicality.)

Mexico itself recognizes the importance of border enforcement and has expelled illegal immigrants within its own borders who came without permission from other countries in Latin America. If they recognize the right of nations to enforce their borders, perhaps they can even be persuaded to pay for the U.S.-Mexican border wall—or at least to make some effort to control the flow of people from their side, making enforcement a bit easier on ours.

And it really is the case that Trump is concerned that immigration be orderly and law abiding, not, as some of the nastiest of his critics have suggested, that he wants to "keep America white" (as though America's population were not already about 30 percent nonwhite, including many nonwhite Trump voters, to the Democratic Party's chagrin).

Remember, too, that while the media talks about the hopes of so-called DREAMers from Latin America and tragically displaced Syrian refugees, there is a real problem of entry to the United States by growing, violent Mexican drug gangs and international terrorist networks linked to ISIS—two groups with little in common besides their desire to skirt American law and their fondness for beheading people.

I doubt even left-wing Democrats really believe these things are nonissues and that border security is a trivial matter, but saying so gives them one more issue to hang around Trump's neck to make him sound narrow-minded. I don't think most Americans are falling for it anymore. I don't think people coping with terrorism in Europe, Africa, and the Middle East are falling for it, either.

Turning what could be practical, centrist issues into extremely heated, divisive ones has become a recurring problem in the Swamp. One of the most basic reasons Americans turned to Trump with a mixture of hope and desperation is that we've spent decades now thinking that nothing can be done unless something big changes in the Swamp. For years, no real budgets were passed—just "continuing resolutions" that rubber-stamped minute changes in already-existing budget patterns. The arrival of automatic budget cuts dictated by law is about the biggest progress Congress made on such issues in the decade preceding Trump's arrival. Even those cuts didn't stick.

In the broader culture, which has come to look all too much like an extension of the Swamp as politics reaches into every inlet and rivulet of our lives, every disagreement now becomes fodder for an online war in which you risk being declared either a "fascist" or an "SJW" (a so-called social justice warrior, looking for racism and sexism lurking everywhere) by the other side.

Trump may not be a standard-issue conservative, and he's definitely not a typical liberal like the ones I see around me in New York City every day. But that's exactly why he may be the man who can do another big, seemingly impossible thing that needs doing: Someone has to end the gridlock in Washington.

America has for the past few decades been like a ship drifting inexorably but unnecessarily toward a huge iceberg, and that iceberg is the global collapse of confidence in the dollar if we end up just inflating our way out of the colossal federal debt (with China and Russia more than happy to try becoming the printers of competing reserve currency, dreaming of ending the years of oil prices being defined in dollars). Little by little, inflation has been our preferred method of easing the debt bind in the past. That's what so-called quantitative easing is—artificially low interest rates at the Federal Reserve and some other Western nations' central banks.

Congress's periodic raising of the debt ceiling is greeted with sighs of relief by legislators and the media but should be no more reassuring to the rest of us than a happy thumbs-up from the captain when that hypothetical ship is drifting toward an iceberg, as he assures us he won't be making any sudden, jerky course corrections that might cause us to spill our drinks. Keep drinking as if all is well!

Big, tough decisions have to be made, and soon.

You might have hoped they'd all be handled on Reagan's watch, and he indeed helped point us in the right direction, but it was only a start, and deficit spending increased even as he counseled aiming for spending cuts and fiscal sobriety.

George H. W. Bush merely coasted on Reagan's success, fiscally speaking, not wanting to look too harshly conservative, like his (somewhat populist) predecessor. He should be so lucky!

Bill Clinton actually reduced the deficit, without making much dent in the debt, but the hidden warning sign in his success was that it was more a side effect of gridlock than an overcoming of it. Bill had no shortage of ideas for new spending programs—he rattled them off in nearly every speech he gave. And then a Gingrich-led Congress ignored them. Lucky for him and his legacy, much like Hillary's disastrous and bureaucratic health care plan being blocked by Congress in 1993.

Under George W. Bush, not only did two expensive wars begin but domestic spending increased by over a third, the fastest it had gone up since LBJ. This is conservatism? If so, it had just become one more big-spending part of the Washington establishment. President Trump must rein in spending!

Obama talked hope and change, but he really changed very little—unless you count him quietly letting the debt nearly double, even without proposing any radical-sounding new spending plans aside from his vague "stimulus" that poured money on the problem; bad investments are like using gasoline to put out a fire.

Something has to change, and waking up Congress to the severity and urgency of the problem would be a good start. Trump must ring the fire alarm, because our government is on fire—we are unsustainable if we keep going down this path.

If local knowledge is more effective than trying to learn from a distance in the abstract, maybe a good wake-up call for Congress would be an 80 percent salary cut. If, as suggested in a prior chapter, we're going to have a part-time legislature anyway, they shouldn't complain too much about being paid less. Now, the slimier of the older, longer-term legislators might just react by leaning more heavily on their pals in industry and the nonprofit sector to provide them freebies. But the salary cut could send a powerful signal to freshman legislators that the Swamp is not a place you should go to get rich. How about a lifetime ban on lobbying? Politicians shouldn't be able to enrich themselves on the work that they claimed they were doing only for their constituents.

Citizen legislators who are genuinely there to improve things, not to line their pockets or their cronies' pockets, are the ideal. For years, we haven't dared hope that such legislators, who existed in the earliest days of the republic, could ever walk among us again. Let's try.

There are little signs of hope here and there in Congress already. Senator Rand Paul of Kentucky, a Republican who leans libertarian, is one of the few members of Congress who give back money from the annual allowance all senators receive for all manner of miscellaneous expenses on top of their already-substantial $174,000 salaries. There are three tiers for the expenses, called Members' Representational Allowances (MRAs), based on the size of the officeholder's state, and like many budget items in the Swamp, they work on a "use it or lose it" basis. There's no real incentive not to spend your whole MRA, because it will just vanish back into the maw of the general treasury and who cares about the general treasury—oh, unless you're one of those rare legislators like Paul who actually worry about the overall fiscal health of the nation instead of just feathering their own nests.

And so the end of the allotted MRA period (again, like so many other budget items in government) sees a frenzy of pointless, last-minute spending. Better than losing it! Suddenly, every congressional staffer within reach gets a free set of Bose headphones, or maybe fancy standing desks, extra laptops, or other grand gestures that, of course, aren't really acts of generosity, merely one last bit of fun at the expense of the robbed taxpayer. Trim this. Trim everything, please.

And can I get a big *amen* for President Trump for donating his entire salary to good causes? That act alone is a first step to draining the Swamp. Trump is the first elected official I have ever heard of doing that—and doing so from the Oval Office is both symbolic and a warning shot. Sure, Trump can afford to donate his $400,000-per-year salary, but he really fulfilled a campaign promise by doing so. Many other rich elected officials also could have donated their taxpayer-funded salaries, but none I know of actually have (New York City mayor Mike Bloomberg agreed to a $1 annual salary, though). The warning shot should be heard throughout the Swamp. Trump means business, and his business has always been to drain the Swamp. Be warned, Swamp creatures, the comfort and cover of the murky Swamp waters may evaporate under Trump!

The Swamp creatures constantly chastise normal Americans for being "greedy," for lacking the Swamp creatures' heartfelt concern for the future. Yet it's the perverse incentives of the Swamp, where nothing is really being earned and everything is nonetheless being spent (or at least 40 percent of everything in America, if you count state and local government spending as well), that show us exactly what not to do if we want to live in a world of responsible spending and farsighted frugality.

It's not always the individual Swamp creatures' faults. Scandal-prone as they are, they're just awash in cash they don't know what to do with. How would they? They don't have customers to service. They don't have competitors to fend off with extra hustle or better ideas. They have big, hard-to-track budgets that are thrown at broad, vague problems such as "poverty" or "global tensions" or "urban blight." It's not surprising if they start telling themselves, as any of us might with $4 trillion worth of ways to be lazy, that pretty much anything they do counts as a blow against those problems, even if an ungrateful public sometimes has a hard time seeing how.

And so, for instance, you get members of Congress—and their staffs—discovering that they need to go on "fact-finding junkets," usually not to the middle of a war zone, of course, but maybe someplace exciting like Hawaii or Paris. I mean, sure, there's always a reason. Maybe they need to have a conference with other world leaders. And if so, why not do it at a ritzy, five-star hotel in Switzerland instead of a room in the basement of a congressional office building back home? Probably, they won't learn anything they couldn't have learned from a conference call or, even more efficiently and frugally, email, but they can pretend they "met the people" or looked at "the facts on the ground."

Oh, and they picked up some great souvenirs for their spouses. Or maybe they even brought their spouses on the junket. It's a fun time for the whole legislature! For the taxpayers, not so much. How about a moratorium on nonessential international travel for all government officials?

As a result of this loosey-goosey attitude toward your money, there've been cruises to Europe for the Senate, trips to Hawaii for the House, and even champagne-soaked parties in Vegas for the General Services Administration a few years ago. Yes, the GSA—that would be the nonglamorous little arm of government that's supposed to be in charge of making sure federal government expenditures are being processed properly.

And by the letter of the law, of course, they are! How reassuring! Every dime has an excuse, usually. An excuse—not necessarily a productive purpose. Unless you were lucky enough to get invited to

the champagne party. Or the European cruise. Or get some of those sweet Bose headphones. Did you?

Maybe it would be better if the office budgets in the Swamp were cut so much that they don't even have air-conditioning—just until they eliminate the federal debt, let's say. That seems fair.

But this is rather gloomy talk. Let me outline a more positive vision now before you despair completely.

CONCLUSION

Drain the Swamp, Mr. President. Drain the Swamp.

—ERIC BOLLING

The nation's Founding Fathers may have put the capital city in a literal swamp, but they did not want it to become the moral and political Swamp with which we live today. What did they envision?

For one thing, the framers of the Constitution did not envision the central, federal government wielding great power over the states, let alone the details of every individual's life. The Founding Fathers knew that mankind is susceptible to our own desires, power, money, sex, and influence, and they wanted the central government strictly limited because of it. They had just escaped the British king, and most of them had no desire to replace the British king with an American one.

The Founding Fathers may have thought more like lawyers (which many of them were) than like philosophers, but that worked out for the best. Though Thomas Jefferson had laid out a very philosophical description of individual rights in the Declaration of Independence, even that document was a litany of specific, concrete complaints about misdeeds by the Crown. The Constitution, even more so, reads like a practical compromise hammered out by lawyers representing competing interests, not just one arrogant know-it-all's conception of good government or the good life.

The Founding Fathers trusted in checks and balances between the three branches of government—and state-versus-federal tension between governments—to stymie people's most sweeping and dangerous governing impulses.

In essence, rather than dream idly of a perfect government or perfect world, the Founding Fathers foresaw the high likelihood of Swamp behavior and through compromise and strict rules hoped to keep that behavior at least partially contained. You can't really turn the Swamp into a beautiful garden, I'm afraid, but you can put strong walls around the Swamp that keep it small.

The Constitution, by carefully spelling out the very few functions that the central government is supposed to have, and its deference to the states on most matters, was an exercise in Swamp management. The Founding Fathers cannot travel to our time and drain the Swamp for us, but they tried to help us out, across the centuries, by making the conditions for the Swamp's growth poor in the first place. Instead of feeding its vines with vast unenumerated powers, they gave us a Bill of Rights that is essentially a long list of things the federal government cannot do, ways in which the Swamp is forbidden to expand.

They also intended the Ninth Amendment to make clear that the Bill of Rights was by no means all the rights that individuals have. We have the right to do virtually anything not spelled out in the Constitution as an area of life over which the federal government has specific authority. Over two centuries of constitutional law have evolved in the interim, but the default assumption should still be that we have freedom whereas the Swamp has strict limits. It is action by the government that must be justified by pointing to its authorization in the Constitution, not our life choices.

The Founding Fathers knew that a republic is a fragile thing, that all prior experiments with republican (small *r*) government had eventually failed. Their vision of government was (by the standards of big-government advocates) unambitious not because they were callous or unimaginative but because they knew how many different ways government could go wrong. Don't let the Swamp get too thick and overgrown and it will be less apt to hide monsters.

If the government just runs courts that punish robbers and violent criminals, plus a strong national defense to keep the peace (without roaming the earth looking for new fights), it will have plenty to do, the Founding Fathers will have fulfilled their mission, and American citizens can get on with their lives.

In the twenty-first century, not many people remember the crucial founding idea that government was meant to be kept small and constrained, but there are a few of us keeping the old faith. No one is claiming that everything was better in the eighteenth century—far from it. But they knew a few things about the perils of governing that we've mostly forgotten.

There are still liberals who are serious about protecting individual liberties, conservatives who look with suspicion upon big government as a sort of phony replacement God, and libertarians who oppose legal encroachments at nearly every turn. The libertarian-leaning conservative writer and radio host Mark Levin gets it. He composed a list he called his "Liberty Agenda," changes we could make today that would restore the best parts of the original American system.

Among other things, his suggestions (with my additions) include:

- Impose congressional term limits (I wholeheartedly agree, as discussed earlier)

- Require a balanced federal budget (works for households)

- Limit spending and taxation (as the saying goes, "Taxation is theft")

- Have sunset provisions so that regulations and departments must be reviewed and renewed if they are indeed still considered useful (don't just assume)

- Make it easier for states to amend the Constitution without Congress (the central government is less likely to care about everyone else's independence)

- Allow a vote by two-thirds of the states to overturn any federal law (repeal is good)

What all suggestions of this sort have in common is a recognition that the quality of a government is determined in large part by the procedures according to which it operates. The people we elect will not always be wise. Their decisions will not always be correct. No matter which party and which philosophical faction you hail from, you will sometimes be on the losing side of a given policy. But at least we can limit the harm, decrease the odds of the central government just running amok, by having unassailable procedures in place that tell government: You are not the last word.

> Amendment procedures can stop you.
> The individual states can stop you.
> Individuals' rights can stop you.

The underlying idea at work in all legal and philosophical approaches like that is limited government. That's not an idea that comes naturally to most people, not even in the country founded on the idea, the United States.

What most people would prefer to believe—everyone from the

intellectuals in prestigious colleges to some idiot mouthing off in a bar—is that all you need to do is figure out which things in the economy or the culture we like and which ones we don't, then have government give money to the things we like and make the things we don't like illegal. That sounds "simple" to most people. You're sick of rap music? Ban it! You think grocery store clerks should make more money? Pass a law that says now they do! Presto! Easy!

But not only do all such laws have unintended consequences (such as a lot of angry rap fans and lots of layoffs by grocery stores that can no longer afford to pay their clerks), they add up over time to create bureaucracy, making it hard to navigate any new way of doing things. Then, even if your intentions sounded modest and reasonable, you've moved the country away from freedom and into totalitarianism. Maybe you didn't want Stalin—you never voted for crackdowns on dissidents—but you've turned our legal world into a maze in which there's no room left for individuals to disagree with the crowd.

I suspect part of the problem is that most people don't really ever expect to wield political power. They're like limited government believers at heart because they just want to go on managing their own individual lives. So when the rare opportunity arises to think politically—when an opinion poll firm or a political campaigner calls them up—they start indulging their fantasies. They do it without stopping to ask, "Wait, do I really know anything about politics or economics?" It's fun.

It's about the same as when the idiot on the barstool says, "There ought to be a law!" Does he mean that, seriously? Or is he just using a traditional formula for telling you, "This is what I like, and next I'm gonna tell you what I don't like"?

Unfortunately, whenever the public indulges in such fantasies, the Swamp creatures are there, listening. Most of them are such cynics that they know very well the public has not clearly thought through the costs and benefits of the policies the public is spouting off about—but the Swamp creatures don't care! They just need to look like they're responding to the public's whims.

Or at least, the Swamp creatures need to look responsive enough not to be turned out of office in the next election so that they can continue enjoying their perks and doling out favors to their friends. For individual members of Congress, that doesn't even necessarily mean keeping track of general public moods. Remember, unlike a president, each member of Congress basically just has to keep one district (or for senators, one state) happy in order to get returned to the comfort of the Swamp lifestyle each election cycle.

Smart Swamp creatures will avoid even displaying any particular political philosophy or specific policy goals—unless a clear majority of people in their district demand it. Why bother committing yourself to abolishing the wasteful Department of Education or reforming the system for awarding defense contracts if the only topic setting your district on fire is, say, guns (one way or the other) or spending on after-school programs or for that matter literal sagebrush fires? Most Swamp creatures are making the one or two clearcut noises they have to and are otherwise keeping their heads down, unless they decide to run for office or think they might one day. There are huge risks to taking a clear stand, after all.

Best to just keep lurking right at the surface, watching for easy opportunities, a bit like an alligator. There aren't too many proud, dignified lions dwelling in the Swamp.

So the mess we've come to know as our big, gridlocked government isn't really the result of one totalitarian master plan. It's the slow accumulation of ideas that helped out one campaign one year, or pleased one district a few decades ago, or "sounded good at the time" in one impassioned (or pretend-impassioned) speech on the House floor that played well on TV. It's the slow, sedimentary growth that occurs when no one is paying attention, no one is making the tough decisions, and each member is just hoping the debt/spending imbalance can gets kicked a little farther down the road before a big, ugly reckoning comes.

Perversely, the bigger government gets, though, the less likely it becomes that any one of these creatures is going to stick his neck out and alter the whole system. On the contrary, the bigger it gets, the more opportunistic bacteria crowd into the Swamp, seeing chances to suck up a little subsidy over here, tweak a regulation to help a buddy over there, appoint some pals to a cushy office over there.

Think about how people tend to behave even in private bureaucracies. When there's not much chance of being noticed, even halfway-decent people at some point say, "Why bother trying to fix things? No one seems to care, so I might as well get my share. Maybe the Department of Commerce is hiring. Easier than starting a real business."

That's how you end up with a continually expanding Swamp.

Contrast that, if you will, with the natural sense of personal responsibility that most Americans exhibit in their everyday lives. You know you can't just walk over to your neighbor's house and take his money if you run out of your own. You can't just annex the neighbor's garage because you think you have a better, more socially enlightened use for it than your neighbor does.

The left will say that individuals in the marketplace are greedy and self-absorbed, but if they abide by the rules of the marketplace, including basic respect for property rights—"Thou shalt not steal"—there is a very serious limit to their greed. People in the marketplace must pay for what they use. They must trade their labor or products or the goods they already own for what the other person is willing to offer. That, not the latest government committee report or ponderous speech, is what keeps most human beings on the straight and narrow and makes them productive citizens.

There will be people who need our help and genuinely cannot produce enough to flourish in the market, but in a market freed from most regulations and taxes, there will be more than enough wealth to take care of them—and probably even new opportunities for them to work or invest that we never thought of before. There always are, once people are liberated to look for them.

Don't let the Swamp creatures lure you into their domain by claiming that they're the only ones looking out for the poor and the downtrodden. The Swamp creatures use the poor and downtrodden to justify their own existences, as befits natural parasites.

But then, I am not worried that we are all fragile creatures on the brink of collapse without the Swamp creatures to "help" us. Despite all the horrors of government described in this book, I am fundamentally an optimist.

Optimism isn't just a personal outlook, an expression of some people's temperament. A nation can be optimistic or pessimistic as well. Has there ever been a more optimistic creed than "life, liberty, and the pursuit of happiness" described in the Declaration of Independence? Europeans colonized North America because they believed they could do better, earn more, build more here breathing free air than back in the Old World worrying about the monarchs' decrees.

Optimism is the faith that leads to innovation, to achievement, to prosperity. It was true in the time of the colonists, and it's true in the early twenty-first century if we don't let the voices of doom make us forget. America is the greatest nation on earth, and our lawmakers must protect what God has blessed us with. I am optimistic that with the simple, commonsense changes to the way the government works I've described in these pages, Donald Trump can drain the Swamp and America can achieve new heights of prosperity.

Throughout the second half of the twentieth century, the United States' annual economic growth rate was over 3 percent. Compare that to the anemic 1.5 percent we saw during the Obama presidency, caused in no small part by the financial crisis but exacerbated rather than lessened by his stimulus spending and new regulations. Remember, as impressive as it may sound for a president to throw around a trillion dollars (of other people's money) in "stimulus," that really just means that money flowed to places that sounded like a neat idea to politicians that could instead have been left to the market to allocate efficiently—to the places where the money produced the biggest return on investment.

Want a real trillion-dollar stimulus suggestion? How about big tax cuts that leave an extra trillion in the hands of private buyers, sellers, and investors who might actually know what they're doing?

If instead we keep entrusting government to call the shots, to allocate the resources, to decide which projects will be pursued and which will die on the vine waiting for approvals, not only will the United States remain economically stagnant (the way Europe was for most of the second half of the twentieth century under its big regulatory states), but it will continue to experience political scandals and to become ever less outraged by them.

Why's that? Well, what do you think tends to happen to people who get handed $4 trillion of other people's money year in and year out, the way the 535 members of Congress and their cronies do? Who wouldn't become corrupt if he truly, deeply believed that all that loot was his moral just deserts? Only a rare few. I say we stop tempting those poor Swamp creatures. They're weak. It's their nature. We've seen that in the two centuries' worth of anecdotes in this book and countless other tawdry tales that could be related or found in your daily newspaper.

Big government and the corruption of the Swamp go hand in hand.

In order to drain this Swamp, we're all going to have to apply pressure now, even if this isn't quite the time we expected to fight this battle and this isn't quite the political situation we expected to see during the battle.

A century ago, there were Progressives who believed in making government bigger but also more rational, a well-behaved civil service that would put the good of the nation ahead of parochial or partisan politics. That dream didn't work out. All we got instead was the part about government getting bigger. The "good government" advocates got only government.

In the late twentieth century, there were conservatives who believed that government and the culture as a whole could be slowly, elegantly steered back on course by teaching people more about the classics of Western literature, the fine points of philosophy, and the details of free-market economics, binding all those elements together in a renewed Judeo-Christian ethos. That didn't exactly work out either, I'm afraid.

At the start of the twenty-first century, there was talk of a "libertarian moment" in which it was hoped by some that America would adopt an entire new across-the-board philosophy of government, with nearly everyone seeing merit in smoking pot, opening your own business, or shutting down the Department of the Interior, but somehow the public didn't latch onto that whole philosophy, and maybe they never will take the whole idea in one gulp, though it would address many of the concerns I've expressed here about government overreach.

We can't wait for the whole world to adopt any precise philosophy, though, whether liberal, conservative, or libertarian. That $20 trillion debt looms, the cartels and terrorists are at the door, and jobless Americans are growing extremely impatient. We have a strange, unexpected chance to break with business as usual, the phony business of Washington that hasn't been working, and that unexpected chance is a larger-than-life leader named Donald Trump.

I sure am betting on him to drain the Swamp. He doesn't have to do it alone, though. Let him, your representatives, any press you might talk to, your neighbors, and more know that you take the problem of the corrupt, wasteful Swamp seriously enough to want to see big change and see it now.

Make it clear that we, as a nation, take the problem of the Swamp more seriously than we take the chance to mooch one more small freebie off the system. We take the problem of the Swamp more seriously than the latest pseudoproblem the Swamp creatures claim they'll fix for us if only we give them just a little more power and a little more of our money—as well as a little more of the time that we don't have in our current fiscal situation.

The dirtiest secret at the heart of the Swamp, to tell you the truth, is that for all the noise its inhabitants make, if the Swamp is drained, virtually no one in America outside of Washington, D.C., will miss it.

We'll see new businesses opening up, new jobs being created, whole new industries and technologies arising, and we won't once stop to say, "Wait a second. Are we sure the General Services Administration is well funded enough? Do they have all the champagne they need? Can we really forge ahead without the Export-Import Bank? Are we being taxed enough to help out those giant agribusinesses, or should we still be worried about them? Aren't there more rules I could be obeying?"

We'll walk away from the Swamp in 330 million different directions and pursue 330 million different projects—or combine our efforts as we choose, individually and in groups. We don't need to be mired in one plan that suits the Swamp creatures more than it suits any of us. The Swamp is a moral and economic lowland. We can lift ourselves—and each other—up above it. Greatness really does lie out there, away from the Swamp, in the form of new businesses and new voluntary associations of all kinds, from churches to internet message boards.

Draining the Swamp doesn't just mean some net loss, the way the left would usually have it, as if it's an act of pure destruction. Draining the Swamp means new life-giving fluids flowing to all those other American activities, beyond the D.C. beltway.

If you think big government is a precious resource that we can't do without—one worth enduring all those scandals and colossal policy blunders—at least stop to reflect upon that 40 percent of national income we'd all have back, in nongovernmental hands if, hypothetically, we got rid of government (not that I'm suggesting the whole thing, not quite—but let's try this as a mental experiment for a moment).

Gone would be one or two popular government programs, but might it be more than made up for if, say, you had 40 percent of your income back? Or it was 40 percent easier to start a new firm? Or you benefited from 40 percent more research and development in private labs? Or your struggling middle-class acquaintances were 40 percent richer and thus far more able to perform charity? Can you imagine 40 percent more hardware stores, personal electronics, houses, or clothing options?

Couldn't we make something from all of that, something that more than makes up for the absence of the Department of the Interior or the National Endowment for the Arts? Vast resources are sinking into that Swamp. It's time we took them back.

If we no longer believe that, if we think pessimism is the natural, rational reaction to a changing world and changing economic times, that only immersion in the Swamp can bring us peace, well, then, we can march in deep. Let the slime encircle us up to the neck. Let 535 senators and representatives decide our fates. Let reams of Occupational Safety and Health Administration rules determine which sorts of businesses we'll dream of building and which we won't. Let our children be educated to serve in the bowels of government agencies crunching numbers about how best to redistribute other people's money.

Worst of all, we should then be prepared to let the likes of Anthony Weiner, James Wilkinson, Donald "Buz" Lukens, and that waterlogged embarrassment Ted Kennedy decide our fates. Is that the best we can do? Are they the best we can do? Better then to just give up and sink to the bottom of the Swamp—or drain it for good and build something beautiful where the Swamp used to be.

Draining the Swamp really means taking our individual lives back from those creatures.

Are we so frightened and pessimistic in America in the early twenty-first century that we think we deserve to be subjugated by them? I don't think that's what the Founding Fathers had in mind, and you know what? I don't think it's what liberals, conservatives, libertarians, or anyone else really envisioned even when they made the mistake of looking to Washington, D.C., as the place where our problems would get fixed. Most of us know it isn't where the action is.

That's why so many Americans have lost the ability to take politicians seriously, give thoughtful answers to political opinion polls, and pretend that the narrow range of policy ideas and options offered to us by the mainstream media is what you have to settle for. We know things can be better than this.

I'm an optimist, and creating a better future means always striving to stay out of this Swamp. When President Trump drains the Swamp, America truly will be great again!

Drain the Swamp, Mr. President. Drain the Swamp.

NOTES

3. BRAWLING IN THE HOUSE

34 *despite his change of careers*: J. Stepman, "The Top 5 Brawls in American Political History," BearingsArms.com, October 21, 2012, https://bearingarms.com /jstepman/2012/10/21/the-top-5-brawls-in-american-political-history/.

37 *whole case "in four minutes"*: "To Thomas Jefferson from Albert Gallatin, 31 January 1803" (explanatory note), Founders.Archives.gov, https://founders.archives .gov/documents/Jefferson/01-39-02-0363.

42 *dogs removed from the floor*: Robert V. Remini, *Henry Clay: Statesman for the Union* (New York: W. W. Norton, 1993), 83.

44 *iron-handled cane until it broke*: "Representative Lovell H. Rousseau Assaulted Representative Josiah B. Grinnell," History.House.gov, http://history.house.gov /HistoricalHighlight/Detail/36235?ret=True.

4. FOREIGN ENTANGLEMENTS

49 *That man was William Blount*: Michael Toomey, "William Blount (1749–1800)," NorthCarolinaHistory.org, http://northcarolinahistory.org/encyclopedia/william -blount-1749-1800/.

5. LOBBYING IN THE SWAMP

62 *Samuel Swartwout, skimmed $1,225,705.69*: "Did You Know . . . Samuel Swartwout Skimmed Staggering Sums?" U.S. Customs and Border Protection, https://www.cbp .gov/about/history/did-you-know/samuel-swartwout.

66 *Democratic donors to Russia*: Paul Roderick Gregory, "No One Mentions That the Russian Trail Leads to Democratic Lobbyists," Forbes.com, February 18, 2017, https://www.forbes.com/sites/paulroderickgregory/2017/02/18/no-one-mentions -that-the-russian-trail-leads-to-democratic-lobbyists/#16157a463991.

6. CAMPAIGN OF ERROR

78 *Lincoln's secretary of war, Simon Cameron*: "Simon Cameron Facts," Biography .YourDictionary.com, http://biography.yourdictionary.com/simon-cameron.

83 *Virginia mulatto father*: Kerwin Swint, "Adams vs. Jefferson: The Birth of Negative Campaigning in the U.S.," *Mental Floss*, September 9, 2012.

8. BIG GOVERNMENT, BIG SCANDALS

97 *H. Burd Cassel of Pennsylvania*: "H. Burd Cassel in Scandal: Pennsylvania Inquisitors Ask If Congressman Gave $10,000 Hush Money," *New York Times*, April 30, 1907.

102 *lands surrounding the Grand Canyon*: Douglas H. Strong, "Ralph Cameron and the Grand Canyon (Part I)," *Arizona and the West* 20, no. 1 (Spring, 1978).

105 *before her eyes last night*: Chris Grygiel, "Suicide—or Murder? 75th Anniversary of Pol's Sensational Death," *Seattle Post-Intelligencer*, August 30, 2011, http://www.seattlepi.com /local/article/Suicide-or-murder-75th-anniversary-of-pol-s-1740520.php.

105 *Zioncheck's plunge was the finale of a tragic history of mental illness*: "The Congressman from Crazy Town: Marion Zioncheck of Washington," KnoxFocus.com, April 26, 2015, http://knoxfocus.com/2015/04/congressman-crazy-town-marion-zioncheck -washington/.

9. WAR MACHINE, SCANDAL MACHINE

107 *Humvee window installations*: Joe Mandak, "Defense Contractor: Former Owners, Exec to Blame for Scheme to Overcharge Warren-Based TACOM," Associated Press, March 6, 2017, http://www.crainsdetroit.com/article/20170306/NEWS01 /170309904/defense-contractor-former-owners-exec-to-blame-for-scheme-to.

107 *quarter million dollars' worth of medical equipment*: Mark Saunders, "Ex-Defense Contractor Pleads Guilty to Theft of Medical Equipment for Marines," KGTV, March 14, 2017, http://www.10news.com/news/ex-defense-contractor-pleads-guilty -to-theft-of-medical-equipment-for-marines.

109 *military doesn't judge worth funding*: Matthew Cox, "Pentagon Tells Congress to Stop Buying Equipment It Doesn't Need," Military.com, January 28, 2015, www .military.com/daily-news/2015/01/28/pentagon-tells-congress-to-stop-buying -equipment-it-doesnt-need.html.

109 *tell the Pentagon it was wrong*: Martin Matishak, "Senators Push Back Against Proposal for More Base Closures," TheHill.com, March 11, 2015, http://thehill.com/policy /defense/235397-senate-lawmakers-skeptical-about-base-closure-proposal.

10. FROM GREAT SOCIETY TO -GATE SOCIETY

118 *break-in and an assassination threat*: Randy Dotinga, "Behind Nixon's Big SD Scandal," VoiceofSanDiego.org, October 7, 2010, www.voiceofsandiego.org/topics /news/behind-nixons-big-sd-scandal/.

120 *in 1967 for financial misconduct*: Dirk Langeveld, "Thomas J. Dodd: Dined and Downed," *Downfall Dictionary*, June 13, 2009, http://downfalldictionary.blogspot .com/2009/06/thomas-j-dodd-dined-and-downed_13.html.

123 *population as "Canucks"*: Bruce Schulman, *The Seventies: The Great Shift in American Culture, Society, and Politics* (Boston: Dea Capo Press, 2002), 45.

124 *investigating the IRS*: Amy Handlin, ed., *Dirty Deals? An Encyclopedia of Lobbying, Political Influence, and Corruption* (Santa Barbara, CA: ABC-CLIO, 2014), 380.

124 *gold in them there hills*: Gail Russell Chaddock, "Playing the IRS card: Six Presidents Who Used the IRS to Bash Political Foes," *Christian Science Monitor*, May 17, 2013, http://www.csmonitor.com/USA/Politics/DC-Decoder/2013/0517/Playing-the -IRS-card-Six-presidents-who-used-the-IRS-to-bash-political-foes/President -Richard-Nixon-R.

125 *so-called Abscam sting*: Ted Sherman, "Jersey Hustle: The Real-Life Story of Abscam," *Inside Jersey*, November 25, 2013, www.nj.com/inside-jersey/index.ssf/2013 /11/jersey_hustle_the_real-life_story_of_abscam.html.

11. A REPUBLICAN SOAK IN THE SWAMP

129 *efficient and timely manner*: Ronald Reagan, "Radio Address to the Nation on Waste, Fraud, Abuse, and Mismanagement in the Federal Government," May 5, 1984, archived by the University of California–Santa Barbara, www.presidency.ucsb.edu /ws/?pid=39863.

12. CONTRACT WITH AMERICA, CONTACT WITH AN INTERN

140 *The Clintons' time in the White House*: "21 Most Consequential Clinton Scandals, Ranked from Most Important," *Washington Times*, October 12, 2015.

141 *some reason six months earlier*: "Rose Law Firm Billing Records," *Frontline: Once Upon a Time in Arkansas*, PBS.org, www.pbs.org/wgbh/pages/frontline/shows /arkansas/docs/recs.html.

143 *Sidney Blumenthal were connected*: Lachlan Markay and Brent Scher, "Emails Suggest Clinton Pushed Libyan Business Interests of Off-the-Books Adviser," *Washington Free Beacon*, October 8, 2015, http://freebeacon.com/national-security/emails-suggest -clinton-pushed-libyan-business-interests-of-off-the-books-adviser/.

13. PATH OUT OF THE SWAMP: LIMIT TERMS, LIMIT LOBBYING

147 *arguably corrupt governments*: Mike Hanlon, "Our Rotten World: New Data Shows 85% of Humans Live Under a Corrupt Government," January 26, 2017, NewAtlas .com, http://newatlas.com/2016-corruption-perceptions-index-our-rotten-world /47566/.

153 *cracking down on voter fraud*: Byron York, "When 1,099 Felons Vote in a Race Won by 312 Ballots," *Washington Examiner*, August 6, 2012, www.washington examiner.com/york-when-1099-felons-vote-in-race-won-by-312-ballots/article /2504163.

14. DRAINING BY DEREGULATING

162 *over 170,000 pages long*: Jon Gabriel, "In a Pickle Over Regulations," Freedom
   Works.org, January 13, 2013, http://www.freedomworks.org/content/pickle-over
   -regulations.
170 *"make money off the internet"*: Eugene Kiely, " 'You Didn't Build That,' Uncut and
   Unedited," FactCheck.org, July 24, 2012, http://www.factcheck.org/2012/07/you
   -didnt-build-that-uncut-and-unedited/.

15. DARE TO DRAIN

187 *elected to the Senate from Texas in decades*: Abby Livingston, "To Beat Ted Cruz,
   Beto O'Rourke Plans to Throw Out the Democratic Playbook," *Texas Tribune*,
   March 31, 2017, https://www.texastribune.org/2017/03/31/to-beat-ted-cruz-beto
   -orourke-throw-out-playbook/.

INDEX